# THERAPY FOR YOUR MIND

# A SELF HELP GUIDE

### For

## Emotional, Psychological & Stress Problems

## Paul Craddock DHP

## Disclaimer

This book is intended to complement and support, not replace normal allopathic medicine or medical treatment. If you suffer from any acute or chronic disease you should always seek medical attention from a qualified doctor immediately. The author and publisher accept no liability or damage of any nature resulting directly or indirectly from the application or use of any information contained within this book.

The author and publisher of this book and the accompanying materials have used their best efforts in preparing this book. The author and publisher make no representation or warranties with respect to the accuracy, applicability, fitness or completeness of the contents of this book. The information contained in this book is strictly for educational purposes. Therefore, if you wish to apply ideas and techniques contained in this book, you are taking full responsibility for your actions.

# DEDICATION

To my brother, Charles, who's psychological and
emotional difficulties, ultimately led him to fall upon
his own sword, prematurely ending his life's journey.

To Gemma,

work through this book
and allow it to lead you
to the light and smooth
your lifes Pathway

lots of love from
the Author — Paul

xx

# CONTENTS

# Preface

# Preface

## ACKNOWLEDGMENTS

Rachel Craddock for the front cover design and author's photograph.

# 1. Preface

I experienced a difficult and traumatic childhood and was left to deal with the resulting anxiety, stress, and psychological problems in adulthood. And so, in my late teenage years in the 1980's I embarked on a journey of research and self-discovery to help myself. Mainstream health care was no help however, fortunately for me, I found the alternative methods and therapies that worked for me. So, after recovering, I eventually trained in psychotherapy and hypnotherapy and at one time was running a successful practice from 3 clinics in different towns.

I found that the types of therapy I had experienced personally, helped many people. Just after I started my therapy practice, a lady phoned me saying she was about to jump out of a high window. I managed to persuade her to come for an immediate consultation. After a series of consultations, she made a complete recovery and went on to recommend countless people to me. This was much appreciated as I built my practice!

Having helped many people over the years, I have discovered that the therapy can take a number of sessions. I found that on average it takes about 8 hourly weekly sessions but, in some cases 20 or more. Some of the more severe cases would need considerably more sessions than that. Therefore, there was potentially issues of the patient being unable to afford the continuing cost of the weekly sessions, becoming unable to travel from a distance and not persevering with their therapy to enable a successful outcome.

The aim of this book is, therefore, to make the therapy necessary to help with anxiety, emotional problems, psychological problems and stress affordable and available to everybody. One to one sessions with a therapist are desirable. However, even if you were seeing a therapist, I would expect that you would still be working through the techniques, and therapies in this book which I have specifically written as a self-help guide. I have successfully used the methods outlined in this book extensively myself and with patients. And therefore, I can vouch for their effectiveness.

Please now read the next chapter on "How to use this book".

Paul Craddock 16th August 2020

# 2. HOW TO USE THIS BOOK

*"It isn't what you have, or who you are, or where you are, or what you are doing that makes you unhappy. It is what you think about".* Dale Carnegie

The program in this book is designed to progressively reduce the effects of anxiety, stress and the symptoms of the complete range emotional and psychological problems which humanity suffers from today. If you stick with me and persevere, I would expect you to be able to completely recover from your symptoms. However, even if you are absolutely fine with no stress, anxiety or mental health problems whatsoever, if practiced regularly, you should gain immense benefit from the meditation techniques.

Whilst not used by most mainstream mental health centres and hospitals who tend to favour prescription drug-based therapy, the methods and knowledge in this self-help book has been widely tried and tested throughout the world over many years. Maybe you have tried taking prescription drugs and are now ready to take an alternative more natural approach? If you are currently taking prescription drugs, work through this book but consult your doctor before coming off them.

I would suggest that you work through this book in the order that I recommend. Although, you can refer to the fast help chapter at any time to get immediate help to reduce a negative symptom currently being experienced. The Fast Help chapter is for immediate temporary help and the other chapters worked through in the correct order, are designed to progressively reduce, and then permanently remove anxiety, stress and negative symptoms.

You will see the recommended progression route at the end of each chapter. However, I will cover it in detail here:

Start at the next chapter, the **Initial Consultation chapter**, adapted from my on-site face to face initial consultations I have given over many years. This gives you an explanation and understanding of why you may be experiencing the type of problems you are currently suffering from and the way forward.

After the Initial consultation chapter, next go to the **Journal chapter** where I introduce your journal. This is an essential support tool for you to use as you work through this book and it will become like a good friend! Journaling is a very effective therapy on its own.

Next If you haven't already visited the **Fast Help chapter** go there now to get some immediate help.

After the fast help chapter, regardless of where your symptoms are originating from, you need to go to the **Stress Management chapter** so you can start to work on your stress levels. This will help to start to alleviate any current negative health symptoms you are experiencing. Make sure you download the free audio relaxation session to use with this chapter. See the Appendix for details.

Next work through the **Introduction to Meditation chapter**, the **Meditation Practice chapter** and the **Thought & Emotion Control chapter** in that order. You will then have some amazing tools to remove anxiety, reduce mental health problems, negative thoughts and stress. When you finish the Thought & Emotion Control chapter, the **Spiritual Part Chapter** deserves a visit, it will provide some empowering essential spiritual knowledge whether you are ready for it or not! This type of knowledge forms part of many powerful organisations teachings such as the Transcendental meditation (TM) organisation. Many leaders and well-known celebrities are associated with the Transcendental Meditation Organisation.

Next to get motivated and get a plan so you can look forward in life and set some personal goals, visit the **Personal Development chapter**.

Last but certainly not least, go to the **Memory & Emotion Recall chapter**. In This chapter you will be using a tried and tested technique to permanently remove the type of symptoms covered in the Initial

Consultation chapter. Whilst working through the Memory & Emotion Recall chapter, you should still be partaking in your meditation sessions. Daily meditation practice is a beneficial continuous lifestyle choice. Use the fast help and stress management chapter whenever you feel you need too.

The **Memory & Emotion Recall chapter** utilises a weekly session along with journal work. Use it until you are happy your symptoms have gone or considerably reduced. I will warn you, however, you will need to persist, if you do you will arrive at your ideal destination.

So, there you have it, you have some powerful self-help techniques available, but you must decide right now to work through them continuously. You must persevere, you really must! I cannot emphasise that enough! The alternative is that you are possibly, not going to resolve and completely release the underlying cause of your symptom in order for you to feel much better! So, visualise the outcome you want for yourself and make a commitment with yourself to work towards it. After all, you will only be letting yourself down if you do not!

Ask yourself where you want to be in a year from now? Feeling much better and free from your problem, I guess? So, I want you to imagine two different scenarios: the first one is that you have *not* persistently and consistently worked through this book and have experienced *no* significant improvement.

Now imagine how you will feel about yourself in one years' time if this is the case? Take a few moments to really think about that scenario. Now come back to the present and then go a year ahead in your imagination again. And the situation this time, is that you have persevered and worked through this book and are feeling considerably better.

Having considered how you will feel in a years' time when either you have or have not, persevered and worked through this book. Which path are you going to take? I thought so, I will see you at the Initial Consultation chapter!

*When you are ready, make sure you go to the first page of the Appendix to get support information and download the free relaxation audio.*

Initial Consultation > Journal > Fast Help > Stress Management > Introduction to Meditation > Meditation Practice > Thought & Emotion Control > Spiritual Part > Personal Development > Memory & Emotion Recall

# 3. Your Initial Consultation

*"Most men occasionally stumble over the truth but most pick themselves up and continue as if nothing had happened".* Winston Churchill

This chapter is in the form of an initial consultation which I have undertaken countless times face to face with clients in my consulting rooms. During this initial consultation, I would usually obtain information about their "problem", explain how this "problem" may have arisen and the steps, techniques and methods we need to follow to help them overcome their "problem".

Whilst we may have a slight disadvantage here because you're not sitting in front of me. Because you have chosen to read this book, I already know something significant about you! This is because most people who consult me are either doing something they *don't* want to do or, are *not* doing something they *do* want to do. Another way of putting it would be to say that you are suffering from something inside of yourself but outside of your control. Perhaps, you could also say that you are experiencing a feeling or emotion that you would rather not have, and you have no control over it.

So, you are likely to be suffering from something inside of yourself but outside of your control. This definition covers a multitude of psychological and emotional disorders. This typically includes, anxiety, panic attacks, phobia's, depression and mood disorders, neurotic and psychotic behaviour and compulsive out of control behaviour. If you have a psychotic disorder you are unlikely to be reading this book. This is because a person suffering from a psychosis clearly has something wrong with them. However, they cannot understand this and think that in fact that there is nothing wrong with them. With a neurosis you are aware that you have a problem and are seeking help. I should add that a psychosis is an extreme form of a neuroses. So, I would recommend seeking help whilst you are able too. Because there is a remote but nevertheless real possibility, that if you are unlucky, your neurosis could develop into a psychosis whereby you will not be in a position to seek help because you will think there is nothing wrong with you!

Some clients however, perhaps like yourself, have consulted me maybe suffering from depression anxiety or excess stress as a result of their work, difficult personal relationships or their current stressful personal circumstances. In other words, the current situation they find themselves in is causing their symptoms rather than what has happened in the past in their childhood or from a recent single severe traumatic incident causing post-traumatic stress disorder. It is entirely possible of course, that unresolved issues from the past are adding to life's difficulties currently being experienced making symptoms worse.

If you can clearly identify that a current situation is causing a problem, then my explanation below under "How did I get like this" may not entirely apply to you. but it may to a certain extent! Most of us have at least a certain amount of unprocessed emotions stored from childhood. This may not be noticed and so we are symptom free, until that is, it gets added to by life's current stressful event we are now faced with. In this area of the human condition there are enough grey areas to paint a grey battleship! So, I would suggest that it may be a good idea to read through this chapter to the journal chapter and we will take it from there!

However, do not forget you can visit the Fast Help chapter for fast relief of symptoms at any time. The other chapters are there with the aim to permanently remove your symptoms, so they don't come back. My aim is to get you to the best person you could be if fate had not intervened.

## How did I get like this?

The fact that there is something inside of you but out of your control would suggest that you have previously unsuccessfully expended a vast amount of conscious mental energy trying to overcome your problem. If the problem were in your conscious mind you would have succeeded but it is not, it's in the subconscious part of your mind not directly accessed by your conscious mind. It may be possible to get some limited help from using therapies like CBT using the conscious mind. However, as the source of the problem will be in the subconscious mind the symptoms will not completely be removed and will most likely return.

So, we have (at least) two parts to our mind. Namely, the conscious mind and the subconscious mind. Your conscious mind is the part that you think is you! This part holds your thoughts and reasoning abilities. However, you are unable to undertake more than one activity at the same time. Like reading a book and having a conversation. Your subconscious mind on the other hand, is responsible for running all your bodies processes all at the same time. For example, whilst you are reading this book, your subconscious mind is looking after all your bodily functions at the same time. Therefore, your subconscious mind controls and runs a large number of processes at the same time. It is therefore much more powerful than the conscious mind which can only really focus on one task at a time!

Accepting that if your problem was in your conscious mind that you would have rationalised and dealt with it by now, then it would be safe to assume that whatever the problem is, it resides in the subconscious part of your mind. And as your subconscious mind has control over your body, including its emotions, if something is causing it a problem, it has a vast array of symptoms to choose from to give you! These can include physical symptoms like a nervous twitch or worse! Let us look at the symptoms which can be experienced in an anxiety attack. If you were suffering from an anxiety attack you would not necessary experience all the symptoms listed below:

1. The heart beats alarmingly quickly
2. Increase in breathing rate as if not getting enough air (air hunger)
3. Cramped feeling across lower part of the diaphragm
4. Tingling sensation
5. Hot or cold flush in unexpected parts of the body, usually the extremities
6. Feeling that unconsciousness may be coming
7. Rooted to the spot as if you had seen a ghost
8. Dumbstruck or immobilised
9. Panic struck at what is taken place
10. A return to normal

Examples of your subconscious mind making you behave in an out of control manner would also include any ceremony or ritual about daily habits which are out of the ordinary. Such as washing your hands 5 times before breakfast or turning socks inside out before putting them on. Or walking over every crack in the pavement, for example. Additionally, any silly fears such as heights, flames, knives, rats with long tails, snakes, blood, water, death, darkness, germs, cancer etc.... Also, compulsively keeping checking things and a proneness to blushing. I could go on and will discuss further symptoms your subconscious mind can give you if something is disturbing it later.

# What causes my subconscious mind to give me these symptoms?

Your subconscious mind is there to protect you, and only you. This is because it is *your* subconscious mind! So, what is going on in your subconscious mind? Well it is trying to protect you from something. Something inside of you! let me explain. It has the ability to repress an unpalatable emotion from the conscious mind if the conscious mind cannot deal with it. A person's subconscious will repress it in order to protect the conscious mind.

A person's mind will repress with convenient amnesia something very unpalatable to that person. [i] If the incident had generated an emotion too intense for the conscious mind to process, the subconscious mind will block the memory along with the emotion from conscious recall. Although sometimes the memory can remain, but the emotion has been repressed.

Another way of putting it, is that normally your conscious mind will process emotions as they arise or afterwards. However, if they are of a very intense nature the subconscious mind will repress them from conscious recall to protect your conscious mind. You then have repressed memories and emotions. Or put more simply, you have *unprocessed emotions*. Because your subconscious mind has kept these emotions from conscious recall it experiences anxiety. You can experience this anxiety directly as an anxious feeling within you. Or, by the way of symptom substitution. More about this later.

An example of this would be someone who is involved in a road accident who truthfully tells the police "I remember backing my car out of the drive and remember waking up in hospital. However, I cannot remember the drive to the scene of the accident, or of the accident itself". In order to protect this person's mind from the horror of the accident, this person's subconscious mind has also repressed the memory of the rest of the journey and the journey in the ambulance.

Another example concerns an old patient of mine, this gentleman had been seeing me for around 8 sessions of hypnotherapy to get to the root cause of a problem. At this session he started to recall the originating incident with the accompanying intense emotion. This included intense bodily sensations, which we call an abreaction. Then all of a sudden, the recall stopped. In order to stop the abreaction, I ended the session. He then looked at me and asked whom I was and where he was! Whatever he had started to bring to his conscious awareness was so traumatic and was so painful that his subconscious mine reburied it again. As it did so, he could not remember who I was or where he was. We had to call his wife to pick him up. Fortunately, over the cause of the following week his recent memory slowly returned, and we were able to resume with his therapy. He had had a demonstration of the very mental prosses which had buried the original traumatic event which was causing him anxiety and an associated symptom/problem.

To help illustrate the need for the subconscious mind to repress an unresolved emotion, I will use an analogy. I want you to imagine a large tyre, this is the equivalent of your conscious mind and biological organism. Now imagine using a pump to put air into this imaginary tyre, this air is the equivalent of an intense negative emotion or trauma. The tyre can only take so much air pressure before exploding. Your conscious mind and biological organism can also only take so much of an intensity of emotion or trauma before metaphorically exploding into a complete breakdown. The biological organism can only take so much, and so a safety mechanism is required in that the subconscious mind hides the overload of negative emotion from conscious recall to prevent an overload of the mind and biological organism. However, whilst this unprocessed emotion remains blocked from conscious recall it causes the subconscious mind anxiety.

To further illustrate, I will give you another analogy: Imagine an old-fashioned steam train. See the man on the footplate shovelling coal into the furnace to heat the boiler, now see the large locomotive boiler full of water and steam, the steam which drives the engine. The pressure keeps going up and up. If insufficient steam is not used up in driving the engine, then the pressure builds up inside the boiler. To stop the boiler blowing up under too much pressure, the steam escapes through a safety valve fitted to the top of the boiler. You too have a metaphorical safety valve to stop you metaphorically exploding. In that your subconscious mind can block the excess emotion or trauma that cannot be handled by your conscious mind.

They key here is unprocessed feelings and emotions will produce anxiety. You can experience that anxiety directly as an anxious feeling or the anxiety can be transformed into a symptom. Subconscious anxiety within the human psyche is intolerable to the organism as a whole and will produce an effect on the organism as a whole. Either mentally or physically or a combination of both. This anxiety needs to find an outlet. I am not writing about anxiety as the result of something you are consciously aware of like your job, divorce, family problems, money problems redundancy or bankruptcy, for example. I am writing about anxiety in the subconscious mind. The cause that has been hidden from the conscious mind. Therefore, no amount of thinking about it with your conscious mind will remove the anxiety. Freud talked of free-floating anxiety, nameless, formless, timeless which attaches itself to nothing. The anxiety attack which I have documented earlier in this chapter, is what Sigmund Freud had in mind when he wrote of free-floating anxiety. Meaning it was free of any *known* cause and just literally floated in the mind.

This free-floating anxiety is a problem to the human mind because there is nothing more disconcerting than feeling anxiety and not knowing why. Jung described anxiety as fear spread thinly. Again, there is nothing more disconcerting to the human mind than feeling fear and not knowing why.

## What symptoms are possible?

This anxiety will need to find an outlet. There are different ways this can happen. This is often determined by the personality type of the person concerned. Personality types are determined in our formative years.

### Direct

You can experience anxiety directly, as a strait forward anxious feeling or you can also experience some or all of the components of an anxiety attack listed previously in this chapter.

### Expectant anxiety

This can manifest as a general apprehensiveness, a free-floating anxiety which is ready to attach itself to any idea that is in anyway suitable. It influences judgement, selects what is to be expected, and lies in wait for any opportunity that will allow it to justify itself. This state is called expectant anxiety or anxious expectation.[ii] People who suffer from this kind of anxiety always have a pessimistic outlook on life and see the worst in all possibilities. Where this anxiety is not free floating, it can be bound physically and attached to particular objects or situations. This type of anxiety manifests as a phobia as described below.

## Phobia's

A phobia is an irrational fear and a symbolic representation of the true subconscious anxiety. The list of phobias which people experience is extensive. For a full list see the Appendix. Fear of open spaces, close spaces, of being sick, fear of flying, spiders, mice, blood, snakes, crowds, are few of the common ones. Any irrational fear could be considered a phobia. I am not talking about a response to real and justified danger.

## Externalisation and Identification

The persons anxiety is felt inwardly and projected outwardly. People in the caring professions for example. The unknown has therefore been converted into the known. By removing the troubles of others, the person removes his or her own anxiety.

## Depression

There are commonly two types of depression, namely reactive depression when you are depressed as the result of an external life situation, such as losing your job, the end of a relationship or just fed up with the situation you find yourself in. The other type of depression is clinical depression when you are depressed for no reason, you cannot attribute it to an outside cause. This type of depression has a subconscious cause. As does bipolar disorder where the depression switches to a manic phase. This used to be called manic depression.

## Compulsions

By obsessional actions and compulsions, I am referring to behaviours such as obsessive hand washing or following a particular ceremony, like having to tap a door handle three times before entering or arranging objects in a certain manner, for example. I could give many more examples. The internal anxiety has been diverted and expressed in the obsessional action so the person suffering from these obsessional actions feels no anxiety. However, if the person is stopped from performing their obsessive action or attempt to give it up, they will certainly experience anxiety.

## Addictive Behaviour

Addictive behaviour would be a behaviour which you are unable to control such as gambling, compulsive shopping, being an alcoholic or addicted to sex to the extent of exploiting the other person and probably many people.

## Conversion Disorder

Conversion disorder, also called functional neurological symptom disorder, and previously known as hysteria. It is disorder in which the symptoms or bodily effects cannot be explained by a neurological or general medical condition. Psychological factors, such as subconscious anxiety and conflicts are the cause. Sigmund Freud first used the phrase conversion disorder and hypothesised that the occurrence of certain symptoms not explained by organic diseases reflect unconscious conflict.

The conversion refers to the substitution of a somatic/bodily symptom for a repressed subconscious conflict or emotion.

Examples of conversion symptoms include:

Blindness

Paralysis

Dystonia

Psychogenic nonepileptic seizures

Anaesthesia

Swallowing difficulties

Motor tics and bodily twitches

Speech symptoms such as stammering

Difficulty walking

Someone suffering with a conversion disorder is not feigning the signs and symptoms. Despite the lack of a definitive organic diagnosis, the patient's distress is very real and the physical symptoms the person is experiencing cannot be controlled by their own will and conscious mind. So, the person is not malingering an illness.

Arguably, symptoms like migraine, skin conditions like

eczema and allergies can be included under conversion disorder as the conversion refers to the substitution of a somatic/bodily symptom for a repressed subconscious conflict or emotion. Certainly, anxiety and stress can worsen these symptoms.

## Hysterical Dissociation

Dissociation hysteria is also a manifestation of an underlying subconscious conflict or anxiety. But this is an escape behaviour in which the person gratifies his urges but denies the personal responsibility of his unacceptable behaviour.

## Paranoia

Paranoia is a thought process influenced by subconscious anxiety and typically includes beliefs that they are being persecuted or someone is out to get them. The person can believe that they are threatened or that they are under threat by a conspiracy. Other symptoms include making false accusations and general mistrust of other people. Paranoia is generally a psychotic symptom not a neurotic symptom. So unless you have a mild form of paranoia, as I explained earlier, you would most likely not be aware you are suffering from paranoia and so would not be reading this and if you did, you would think this does not apply to you.

## Post-Traumatic Stress Disorder (PTSD)

This disorder has featured prominently in the news in recent years because of its occurrence in soldiers returning from combat. In world war 1 and 2 it was called shell shock. It may occur in soldiers who have witnessed a traumatic event. PTSD symptoms may include anxiety, excessive vigilance, exaggerated tendency to startle, nightmares, flashbacks to the traumatic event which may be triggered by associated memories, insomnia, outburst of anger and social withdrawal. However Post-Traumatic Stress Disorder (PTSD) can also result from *any* trauma such as being raped or mugged. The intensity of the trauma was too much for the conscious mind to deal with and process and so it remains subconsciously awaiting processing.

**Anxiety and Sexuality**
Anxiety is fear spread thinly. [iii] Fear causes the body to go into the fight or flight response mode directing blood mainly to the essential organs. Sexuality is therefore totally repressed. Imagine a fearful soldier about to jump out of the trenches and go into battle, again sexuality will be the last thing on his mind and totally repressed. Anxiety being fear spread thinly will not totally repress sexuality but, is still likely to inhibit it in some way. I will not elaborate any further but leave it to the readers imagination as to the possible likely inhibitions or restrictions.

Notwithstanding the above, if a person grows up with a lack of love from their parents or parent, the person can develop a low self-worth, have low self-confidence and have a lack of love for themselves. They will therefore find it difficult to love someone else. This of course, can also be an inhibiting factor in relationships.

Lack of love for one's self and repressed emotions as I have covered earlier in this chapter, can result in someone being stuck in a relationship with a partner they don't love. This is because their anxiety prevents them from developing and sustaining a relationship with someone they truly do love. They will often push someone for whom they have deep loving feelings or a great attraction for, away. This is a self defence mechanism in the face of anxiety.

## Out of Control Thoughts

This is a problem concerned with your ego and your conscious mind. The part you think is you, the part you are thinking with right now! Your rational conscious mind is an essential helpful part of you. But it can also get out of control and cause you problems, huge problems! Have you ever woken up in the middle of the night and been unable to get back to sleep because you could not stop your thoughts? Or worse, you couldn't get to sleep in the first place. Do you find you cannot stop thinking about something especially if there is an emotion involved? Do you keep thinking the same thoughts and wonder what's the point I have already thought about this many times? Have you had a disagreement with someone and then keep going over the conversation in your head and then make up a conversation based on what you could have said? Do you start worrying about something and can't stop? All these are common occurrences to humans, you are not alone! The good news is that you can learn how to gain control over your thoughts. It will take some long-term practice but there are also some quick techniques I will teach you in the meantime.

Regarding the long-term practice, I will teach you techniques using meditation. Meditation is a long-term practice, but it gives you a number of benefits. Including enhanced relaxation and a reduction of anxiety, which I guess you need right now!

## Stress

Meditation is guaranteed to reduce stress, but there are also other ways to help and deal with stress. I will discuss these and explain all about stress in the stress chapter. Most of us in the western world suffer from varying degrees of stress and walk around with a certain amount of stored stress day to day. The body is good at storing stress in its muscles, organs and fibres. An analogy of the releasing of stress in the body would be the unwinding of the twisting of the organs and fibres in the body, as the stress slowly releases.

Be sure to move on to the next chapter now (Journal) where we can make a start with your therapy...

Initial Consultation > Journal >

[i] Neil French, Successful Hypnotherapy
[ii] Sigmund Freud 1. Introductory Lectures on Psychoanalysis
Lecture 24, The Common Neurotic State
[iii] Dr C. G. Jung

# 4. Your Journal

*I can shake off everything as I write; my sorrows disappear, my courage is reborn."* Anne Frank

**Advantages of journaling**
There are considerable advantages to keeping a journal. You will discover that your journal is your friend and therapist. It will be your friend at the end of your pen. Journaling has been used as a form of effective therapy for a considerable number of years. I will guide you through how to use your journal as you progress through this book. You will find journaling forms an essential part of this book.

Journaling records the concerns of the heart mind and soul and as you use your journal you will find it helps to get your thoughts in order. It will help you explore your feelings and beliefs and put you in touch with yourself. Your journal lets you express your thoughts and feelings and is always accessible. It is a form of self-care which helps you to get to know yourself.

Writing about your feelings helps improve your mental health. You will explore emotions and facts and see any unhelpful patterns in yourself and others. Therefore, journaling also helps you understand your relationships and importantly, helps you decide on the right conversations to have with the people with whom you have a relationship with, and thus help avoid damaging conflict. It is therefore helpful in processing intensive relationships and avoiding confrontations.

Journaling will help you to deal with traumatic events and stressful pivotal important times in your life when you have to make major decisions or find your way out of a very difficult situation in your life. You will therefore find that you are able to work through problems and see new opportunities.

Offloading your worries on to paper stops you going over thoughts repeatedly. Have you noticed how you keep repeatedly keep thinking the same thoughts? Writing them down cuts this crazy cycle of activity and helps you make the right decisions and helps you achieve your goals. Gaining control of your thoughts in this way helps stop negative and unproductive thoughts and so reduces stress and anxiety.

Journaling also helps improve your sleep by expressing and releasing negative thoughts and feelings and stops you going over them at night and thus keeping you awake or being unable to get back to sleep.

By regularly reviewing your journal, you can look back on your former self and see how you have evolved. You will be able to make decisions based on accurate recordings of past events and revisit memories that may be flawed in detail or lost in time. This will clarify

your thinking and help track events and projects.
Regularly reviewing your journal will also help with
your therapy.

**How to use your journal**
Journaling should be *private* but, if you are seeing a
therapist it would be helpful to share at least some
parts of it provided that your therapist confirms that all
communication is confidential.

Your journaling should be honest. Do not hold
anything back. Completely express yourself. You may
be less than honest with yourself if you are worried
that someone may read your journal. So, take steps
to keep it safe and private. This may mean using a
locked draw, filing cabinet or safe if you are using a
physical paper journal. Or a password protected App
or software. You can easily lock files in Microsoft
Word. There are also many journaling Apps you can
download on to your phone, both free and paid
versions. Pictures and film can often be incorporated
in electronic journals. However, for all electronic
journals whether on Apps or on your computer, make
sure you back up your files in three different places.
This is what professionals storing files and information
recommend. Also be careful with your password.
Some software will *not* allow you to retrieve and
change your password if you forget it. I can vouch for
this by personal experience!

Do not worry about grammar or spelling and record
the date for each entry. You should aim to get into a

habit of writing in your journal regularly. It helps to get into a routine. So, doing it at the same time or place helps. You may at times have to set aside time for specific projects and aspects of your therapy. However, as soon as you have got into a routine you will find journaling an effortless, helpful, and natural part of your life. It is worth mentioning that some Apps have a built-in reminder that prompts you to regularly write in your journal. This is useful in helping you to develop a regular journal writing routine.

**Journal Sections**
Apart from your general observations which you could record in a daily diary format, it can be useful to divide your journal into sections or headers

1. Daily diary
2. Therapy *journal (to include recapitulation of childhood and important emotional events)*
3. Specific problems & projects
4. Personal development, goals and plans
5. Gratitude journal
6. Business journal

All sections should include a review section

It is good to **review** and look back, to see your former self

# Diary
You can use your journal as you would a daily diary simply to record your observations and interpretation of events. You may find that this could overlap with the sections below. So, you could just write the

header for the relevant section above a particular entry.

# Review Section (for all journal sections)

It's good to regularly review what you have written in your journal. There is no set period of time when you should review. You should review when it feels right for you or do so when your therapy necessitates it. Notwithstanding this, it is best to get into a routine of regularly reviewing at least some sections in your diary. This can be done weekly, monthly or longer. Reviewing is helpful in evaluating what has happened, your progress and is a good tool for planning ahead and setting goals.

## Therapy Journal

I will explain how to use the therapy section of your journal as you progress through this book. However, the therapy journal section needs to meet certain requirements.

- Your therapy journal needs to be factual

- Your therapy journal needs to avoid too much focus on the negative

- Your therapy journal needs to be a positive force

- Your therapy journal needs to train your memory recall

- Your therapy journal needs to support your ongoing therapy

- Your therapy journal needs to record your therapy

## Dream Journal

Use daily when you have a dream to write down. Keep a notebook or your journal by your bed and write down your dream immediately upon waking up as you will forget some dreams upon awakening.

There is no need to interpret the content of your dreams. Writing down the content of your dreams serves to help deal with bringing up repressed memories and emotions and can be useful in assisting with your therapy.

## Historical Recall

This section should ideally be used in conjunction with types of analytical therapy involving memory recall and serves as a basis for assisting with the therapy in this book. I will give full details in the relevant chapter.

## Specific Problems & Projects

Often in life we come up against a major problem or a difficult situation we must deal with. We become very worried about a feared outcome. Write down the worst-case scenario and then accept it. Fortunately, it rarely results in death! Take a few moments to really appreciate how you will feel in this worst-case scenario. And really accept it. So, now that you have accepted the worst that can happen, you will find that you cease to worry about it. Now you should write down all the positive things you can do to make sure that the worst-case scenario doesn't happen.

With a problem and an unresolved situation, you also write down the unresolved problem or unresolved situation in your journal and then write down all the possible options and solutions. Note down the possible end result of each possible course of action. When you have done this, you are best placed to work out your ideal solution to your problem or unresolved situation.

It can be helpful to write letters to people you have unresolved emotions with but not send them.

**Personal development, motivation, goals and plans**
Without motivation you will not get far. And sometimes we know we are lacking motivation on some occasions. Normally, we are planning to do something that we know is the right thing to do but feel ourselves lacking in motivation. It could be that you are seeking the motivation to continually use the therapy outlined in this book! Here is a journaling technique to give you the motivation you may need. Use it whenever you need too.

Pick a time when you will not be disturbed. Sit down with your journal in front of you, close your eyes and go ahead in time. The period of time varies with the thing you need to do. So, for an example, let us say you have a mental, emotional or psychological problem you need to resolve. In other words, there is something inside of you but out of your control. Now go ahead one year in time and see that you have not stuck to your therapy program, and nothing has changed for you. Imagine where you are sitting in one year's time still feeling like you do now, but worse, because, you realise you *could be* feeling much better now! Imagine where you will be and how you would be feeling. *Now write it down.*

When you have written it down, clear your mind and close your eyes again and this time, imagine yourself one year ahead, but this time, you have persevered with the therapy and you are looking back feeling good, free of your problem and very proud of yourself. Open your eyes and write down your feelings should this be the outcome in one years' time.

Now understand how you will feel in one years' time as the result of each of the two outcomes above. And decide what path you would like to take. Based on the outcome of how you will feel in one years' time when either you stick to your therapy program or you do not.

Another example could be a diet or stopping smoking. Imagine how you will feel in a years' time if you have stayed with your diet or remained a non-smoker. Then imagine how you will feel in a years' time if you give up your diet or start smoking again.

The key thing is to go ahead in time and compare

how you will feel as the result of doing something or not.

# Gratitude journal

Getting into a habit of writing down something you are grateful for into your journal on a regular basis will help you view life in a more positive way and is especially helpful in tough times. You will find that being grateful for something, will attract more positive things into your life. You will find there is always something in your life that you can be grateful for. That can be very small somethings to very large somethings! There are a considerable number of gratitude journal Apps available.

# Business journal

Richard Branson keeps a business journal, starting right from his earliest days in business, according to his autobiography. It is a great tool for capturing ideas, making plans, and evaluating projects and setting goals. I will not go into any more detail here as its outside the scope of this book. Suffice it to say a separate business journal is a great tool, especially if you are self-employed or run your own business.

Back to your therapy journal … **It is time to start your therapy journal!**

**Therapy Journal exercise. Exercise 1**

Obtain a physical journal/notebook or set up your digital journal

Write in your journal what symptoms you are experiencing and what you need help with. Write down how long you have been experiencing those symptoms

Now make a note of the severity of each symptom on a scale of 1 to 10. With 1 very slight and 10 the most severe.

Now go to the fast help chapter and find ways to get immediate help with your symptom/s and write in your journal how you got on.

**Initial consultation > Journal > Fast Help >**

# 5. Fast Help

*"We tend to forget that happiness doesn't come as a result of getting something we don't have, but rather of recognising and appreciating what we do have."*

Frederick Keonig

In this chapter I have documented various ways in which you can control negative thoughts, emotions and feelings relatively quickly.

## Stopping debilitating thoughts

The best way to gain control over your thoughts and in turn your emotions, is to practice meditation as taught in this book. It takes time, but you will gain control of your inner dialogue and be able to stop it when you need too. In the meantime, there are some techniques you can use below:

The techniques to stop your thoughts described in the meditation section of this book are equally effective outside your meditation session. So, I will go over them again here:

# The Pause Button

Imagine, a pause button symbol represented by two parallel lines of the type found on a video or audio device and its corresponding remote control. Now think back on how you have used such a pause button to pause a film or movie you were watching. When you did this, you were able to see the film frozen on the screen. You were just left with a still image on the screen.

You can do the same with your thoughts. Simply, imagine an exceptionally large pause button symbol represented by two parallel lines superimposed over your thought. Now see your thought frozen just like when you paused a film on your TV phone or computer screen. Really concentrate on this pause button symbol superimposed over your thought, see it clearly in your mind's eye. This will stop your train of thoughts. If thoughts are frozen, they lose their power to continue. Their power is in their movement. Stop their movement and you have control over them. Repeat this procedure as often as you need too.

# The I am responsible affirmation!

Using the principal above that if thoughts are frozen, they lose their power to continue and if you stop their movement you have control of them. A simple affirmation/statement which you repeat to yourself also works. This is "I am responsible" this means that you are saying to yourself "I am responsible for my thoughts". To start with, this will be very difficult to say. You will find yourself saying it through gritted teeth! However, if you persist and repeat this affirmation, it has the effect of freezing the movement of negative thoughts and so they lose their power and you gain control of them. This is because this affirmation removes the power from a negative thought and its associated emotion.

**Other techniques for stopping thoughts:**

# The fan

In your imagination or mind's eye, see a very large electric fan with its blades turning around in front of you. Now imagine walking into that fan, with its blades moving through the inside of your head scrambling and chewing up your thoughts. Take your time to vividly visualise this in your mind's eye. See those unwanted thoughts being shredded and broken up by the blades as they whirl around.

# Further techniques for stopping thoughts:

- Without changing the content of your thoughts try to form them into a rhyme

- Make a song using the contents of your thoughts

- Think backward

- Think in a foreign language that is unfamiliar to you.

- Assign a number to each letter of each word of your thoughts, then add them up to determine the numerical result of your thoughts.

- Go through the multiplication tables

- Recite a prayer from a religion that is not your own

- Try to imitate the form of a well-known comic, using the contents of your thoughts as the material.

## Walk in nature

Being in nature is a good way to relieve stress, anxiety, and mental health issues.

Just 20 minutes in a place such as a park or beach can make a significant difference. Try to make this a regular occurrence. Once a week such as on weekends, I would suggest much longer periods where perhaps you can get more deeper into nature. In times of stress this can be a truly healing experience. I can personally confirm this! Indeed, I have come across a number of cases where a person has been suffering from a severe debilitating mental illness and out of desperation, they have literally moved to live in a remote place in nature. Subsequently, they have seen their symptoms disappear and not return. This often works well in conjunction with getting in spirit or being inspired as described below.

# Get in spirit / inspired

We all need a purpose in life and so take your time to think what inspires you. By that, I mean you need to find an activity, hobby or vocation that gives you an intense satisfaction. You could be living your dream like the lady who moved from the UK to set up and run a kite surfing school in a sunny foreign location to virtually eliminate her severe depression. But you do not necessarily need to go that far!

You simply need to find something to do, such as a hobby that you love, something that you like to do. Something that makes you feel good that you can immerse yourself in. It is probably something that you are good at. Something or an activity that you really look forward to. It is different for everyone. Think back in time, what have you enjoyed doing? What hobbies did you have? What hobby would you like to have? It could be an active one like hiking or a passive but creative one like drawing or painting. If you can enjoy creating something as a hobby, that also certainly works. Being involved in something that gives you pleasure and makes you feel good, being creative doing something which gives you satisfaction is a great antidote to negative feelings and emotions. So, what will you do? Do it now!

# The Calm Technique

This technique is covered in the stress chapter. But here it is again in clear short steps:

When you need to stop a panic attack or to calm down and relax quickly. Stop what you are doing and take a big deep breath, hold it whilst counting silently to 3. And then slowly let it out. Repeat this for a total of 3 times. It is an amazingly simple quick and effective technique. I have broken it down into two steps below. So, try this right now!

**Do the following 3 times consecutively:**

Take a very deep breath and then hold it as you slowly count from 1 to 3.

At the count of 3 slowly let out all of your breath to completely empty your lungs.

# Emo-Trance

This method was developed by Dr Silvia Hartman and is described in her book Oceans of Energy. The Patterns & Techniques of EmoTrance, Volume 1, published in 2003. It is beyond the scope of this book to describe how it works. For this you will need to read her book! However, you just need to understand the technique for it to be effective. Just like you do not need to know how the inside of a television works in order to watch it.

Whilst she wrote a book on the subject, the core

technique is very simple and effective in a matter of minutes. However, I must warn you, this technique will make no sense to the conscious rational part of you. But that is fine, because it does not need to. This is because it works at a deeper energetic subconscious level of your body. So whilst when I describe the technique you need to follow, you may think this is nonsense it doesn't make any sense, I am asking you to suspend your conscious judgment and just go along with it.

I have used Emo-Trance effectively on myself and with countless patients over a long period of time. I can vouch for its effectiveness in quickly removing painful emotions and feelings. I would suggest rehearsing the technique in your mind before you need to use it. So that you fully understand the sequence and so have the technique ready to use if you have not got this book to hand.

## The Emo-Trance Technique

To start with you will have a feeling or emotion that you want to eliminate. For example, anger, guilt, panic, depression, anxiety apprehension, sadness, or fear. This could already have manifested in an area of your body and be expressing itself as a sick feeling or a tightness. It could also be a clear physical pain such as a migraine. It may not be instantly apparent as to where exactly in your body the feeling associated with your emotion or experience resides. So, the first thing to do is to identify exactly where in or on your body you notice the feeling associated with the negative emotion. So, for example if it is tension, where do you feel it? If it is anxiety, where in your body are you feeling it? Pinpoint the exact spot. If it is a sick feeling whereabouts exactly in your stomach do you feel it? If its tension or pressure, zoom in and locate its centre. You get the idea. Do not think about it too much, just do it!

Once you have located exactly where you are experiencing the feeling, focus in on the area, and observe its boundaries like it is a defined mass of energy which is producing the feeling you are experiencing.

Now, without thinking about the likely answer, ask yourself what colour the feeling/mass of energy is? There is no right or wrong answer. And you must not think about it. Just say the first colour that comes into your mind. Just ask the question and instantly say the first colour that comes into your mind. Remember what I said above, in that it will not make any sense to your rational conscious mind!

Now that you have identified the area, defined its mass, boundaries and colour. See it as a solid colour. This means that your feeling is now defined as something relatively solid with a mass and defined area. Now imagine breathing into this defined area and see your breath breaking up this defined area. So, for example, if it is black like a lump of coal. See your breath breaking it up, as it breaks up see it disintegrating into grains of sand or vapour. In this example, grains of black sand or black vapour.

Now as this solid area breaks up into grains of sand or vapour, notice which way it is moving through your body from its defined area. Do not think about it, just notice which way it is moving out through your body. Notice which path it takes as it exits your body. There is no right or wrong way. Again, do not think about it, just observe.

Now keep breathing into the defined solid area and as you do this, keep visualising the solid defined area breaking up and the coloured sand or vapour moving away from it as it breaks up. And moving through your body in its preferred direction which you just observed. As you keep doing this the feeling/emotion will slowly begin to disappear as this solid defined area breaks up and reduces. Keep breathing into the defined area, observing it breaking up into grains of sand of vapour and moving out through your body in its preferred direction. Eventually, the feeling will completely disappear.

If the feeling or negative emotion later returns, repeat the above exercise in its entirety, don't be surprised if any of the aspects are different such as the area where you locate the feeling in your body, colour and which way it wants to move through your body. This is because sometimes it is a bit like clearing through layer after layer. But your making progress as you get through each layer.

**Here is a summary:**

Locate and identify the specific area in your body where you are feeling the negative symptom, painful feeling or emotion.

Observe its boundaries and see it as a defined mass of solid energy which is producing the feeling you are experiencing.

1. Now, without thinking about the likely answer, ask yourself what colour the feeling/mass of energy is?

2. Now see it as a solid colour.

3. Now imagine breathing into this solid colour and see your breath breaking up this defined area. As it breaks up, see it disintegrating into grains of sand or vapour in the colour you gave it.

4. Now as this solid area breaks up into grains of sand or vapour, notice which way it is moving to exit through your body from its defined area. Do not think about it, just notice which way it is moving out through your body. Notice which path it takes as it exits your body. There is no right or wrong way.

5. Keep breathing into the defined area whilst observing it breaking up into grains of sand or vapour and moving out through your body in its

preferred direction. Until the feeling completely disappears.

As you may have noticed, EmoTrance works at an energetic level within your body and as previously mentioned, makes no sense to your conscious mind. However, persevere because the results can be extremely rewarding.

# Externalisation and identification

Put simply, this involves externalising your negative feeling into a suitable activity. Either mentally or physically or both. Some people with mental health problems will already be doing this because their subconscious mind has discovered this mechanism to help relieve a painful emotion. You may have seen this in people who are workaholics, very keen sports people, people who dedicate themselves to helping a cause. This may not always be their motivation but often is.

# Depression

Depression is a type of inward rage, where your feelings are directed back at you. this means you become withdrawn and inactive and consequently do not feel like doing anything.

The trick is to just do any small thing. Get involved in a small activity starting with just a small externalisation or activity to get your mental process moving outwardly. So, motivate yourself to do just one small thing right now and build on that.

# Guided meditation/relaxation audio

A guided relaxation audio session where you can set time aside to relax, close your eyes and be guided through a relaxation session for around 30 minutes is in nearly every case effective. The effects are usually accumulative as you repeat sessions over a period of time. I have recorded such a session, please see the appendix for details. There are of course, other sources.

# Exercise

I cover exercise in the stress management chapter. However, essentially, when we get stressed the body produces certain chemicals which place the body on alert. In the distant past of humanity, these chemicals were burnt up in action when we either ran from danger or fought it. This mostly does not happen now, so the stress chemicals stay in our body keeping us on alert, keeping us stressed and often making getting to sleep difficult. If you partake in exercise, by that I mean exercise that makes your heartbeat faster. This mimics the flight or fight response and burns up the stress chemicals in your body, enabling you to relax. What type of exercise am I writing about? Any exercise that gets your heart beating faster, such as a run or a swim, exercise bike, jogging on the spot or visit to the gym. This exercise to get your heart beating faster could just be for 10 minutes. So, such an activity after a stressful day at work may work wonders!

# Writing a problem in your journal and working through it

If you have a problem that needs solving. Get it out of your mind and write it down in your journal or on a sheet of paper. Write down all the possible scenarios and possibilities. Write down the worst-case scenario and accept it. Then write out what positive things you can do to avoid the worst-case scenario. You cannot worry about the worst-case scenario anymore because you have accepted it. You are now working positively towards a solution.

# Expressing Gratitude

Using your journal to record what you are grateful for each day is a well-documented, tried and tested way of making yourself feel better. However, you do not necessarily need a journal but, its best to use one for long term benefits. It is a simple principal; it just involves thinking what you can be grateful for right now. It can be anything from a loving partner to a sunny day or a nice flower. No matter how bad you think things are, I can absolutely guarantee you can find something to be grateful for.

Being grateful focuses your mind on a positive aspect of your life. Expressing gratitude by some natural law, will attract more positive feelings and events into your life. But also, importantly, direct your chain of thoughts down a more positive road. Thus, attracting more positivity into your life. Therefore, making you feel better and uplifting your mood.

Try this first thing in the morning to set yourself up for the day. I would strongly advise not listening or watching the news or reading about the news first thing in the morning. It is much better to read something positive and uplifting instead, if your aiming to have a positive mood for the day!

Some people also use a gratitude stone. It is simply a nice small smooth pebble, that you can put in your pocket for the day. Every time you notice it in your pocket it reminds you what you decided to be grateful for that day. Try this regularly for a week what have you got to lose?

# Don't take yourself too seriously!

We are all guilty of taking our selves too seriously, it causes all manner of problems in relating to other people. Next time you find yourself getting impatient or over thinking something, tell yourself to stop taking yourself too seriously!

Finally, Read the story below and try to apply the principal when appropriate and in a situation, which demands it. You can practice it when your next held up in a que, I often do!

### Remember rule number 6

*Two prime ministers are sitting in a room discussing affairs of state. Suddenly a man bursts in, apoplectic with fury, shouting and stamping and banging his fist on the desk.*

*The resident prime minister admonishes him: "Peter" he says, "kindly remember Rule Number 6," whereupon Peter is instantly restored to complete calm, apologies, and withdraws.*

*The politicians return to their conversation, only to be interrupted yet again twenty minutes later by a hysterical woman gesticulating wildly, her hair flying.*

*Again, the intruder is greeted with the words: "Marie, please remember Rule Number 6." Complete calm descends once more, and she too withdraws with a bow and an apology.*

*When the scene is repeated for a third time, the visiting prime minister addresses his colleague: "My dear friend, I've seen many things in my life, but never anything as remarkable as this. Would you be willing to share with me the secret of Rule Number 6?"*

*"Very simple," Replies the resident prime minister. "Rule Number 6 is 'Don't take yourself so goddamn seriously".*

*"Ah," says his visitor, "that is a fine rule."*

*After a moment of pondering, he inquires, "And what, may I ask, are the other rules?"*

*"There aren't any."*

From "The Art of Possibility" Rosamund and Benjamin Zander

Now go to the stress management chapter and also download the free relaxation audio which accompanies the stress management chapter. Details of how to download are in the Appendix .

**Initial Consultation > Journal > Fast Help > Stress Management >**

# 6. Introduction to Meditation

*"Your worst enemy cannot harm you as much as your own thoughts unguarded". Buddha*

## What is Meditation?

There are different types of meditation. But generally, meditation uses techniques to slow down and even stop the constant chatter of the mind and gain control over one's mental processes thus achieving a more relaxed state. Meditation has been practiced in various forms for thousands of years.

True Meditation is not about concentration, although concentration can be used as an aid to learn meditation. Meditation is about being fully present in the moment with a heightened awareness.

Many of the meditation techniques taught today are in fact methods to train the mind to slow down to a state of thoughtless awareness. The state of thoughtless awareness is in fact true meditation. You can nevertheless obtain benefits soon after starting your meditation practice as you begin to gain control over your mind and start to relax and de-stress.

Meditation is about getting to know your true self whilst experiencing deep relaxation. It has been used in schools, businesses, prisons and universities. Many celebrities practice meditation including Jennifer Aniston, Arnold Schwarzenegger, Camron Diaz, Russell Brand, Jerry Seinfeld, Katy Perry, Sky Ferreira, Sheryl Crow and Ellen DeGeneres.

## Two Stages of Meditation

Essentially there are two stages to meditation and depending on the type of meditation used and how you practice it, you may only predominantly experience stage 1.

## Stage 1: Mindfulness

Mindfulness meditation practice can include focusing on an object, staying in the present, paying attention, being non-judgemental, focusing on your breathing and or your body. Being present in your body and observing your feelings. It can also include practicing Yoga and Yoga movements.

## Stage 2: Thoughtless Awareness

Called transcendence in Transcendental / Vedic meditation. Otherwise called the still mind, beyond the thinking process, and the silent mind. When stage 2 is achieved you can still practice mindfulness/thought control during your everyday life. So, stage 1 and 2 can be practiced side by side. The term transcendence can also be used to describe a special state of consciousness that can be attained during meditation that is difficult to put into words. But can be experienced as a sense of euphoria where time ceases to exist, your sense of your body is lost, and you experience a profound sense of connection to all that is and will ever be. People who have been meditating for many years (sometimes only a few months) often say that this state of special consciousness is obtained infrequently and may only last for minutes or seconds. But nevertheless, has a lasting positive effect on their wellbeing. I have infrequently experienced a similar state myself and would describe it as a sense of timelessness and disconnection from my body but, being aware and connected to all that is and all that can be. Well I did say it is difficult to describe, didn't I? It must be experienced!

The mind is like the ocean in that your thoughts are the waves and the ocean is the still mind beneath. Like the waves which sit upon the surface which form only a very small part of the ocean, your thoughts represent only a very small part of your mind. Essentially your thoughts could represent only 1% of your mind. However, most people believe that they are only their thoughts!

So, you will be pleased to learn that your worries, fears, anxiety, negative emotions and the like, are not really you. They are not your true self; they are the false in you. Meditation gives you access to the silent part of your mind, where you can observe this false part of you. You can observe your thoughts and as you develop a sense of self separation you, are able to gain control over your thoughts and in turn your negative emotions.

In an earlier chapter we discussed the conscious and subconscious mind. So, where does meditation fit in? To the conscious and subconscious mind, we can add the superconscious mind, otherwise called your higher self, where the silent but aware part I mentioned earlier resides. To this we can add your Ego. The thinking part of you, the part which you think is you, where your thoughts come from, and you think you are your thoughts don't you? We can place the Ego in the conscious mind.

The term superconscious mind otherwise called your higher self, would suggest a more powerful and resourceful part of you. This is certainly the case. The ultimate aim of meditation is to access this part of your mind. From there you can relax more deeply and get rid of stress and recharge your energy quickly. When you are aware from your superconscious mind you are in a state of self-separation. You are separate from your ego and conscious thinking self and so are able to observe your thoughts. Especially the negative ones. You gain a control over your thoughts so you can stop yourself worrying, for example. From this separated state you can also observe your feelings and emotions. You will come to realise that they are separate from your higher self, you will see that these negative feelings are not the real you, they are the false in you. And what do we do with something we discover is false? We discard it! You will do the same with those negative feelings and emotions. Likewise, you will gain control and disregard the thoughts you would rather not have.

From a spiritual point of view, it is said that your higher self has a much better access to the creator of all that is or God or whomever or whatever higher force you feel comfortable with.

# Benefits of meditation

Observed benefits include:

- Help with mental health problems

- Lower blood pressure

- Reduced stress levels

- Help with sleep

- Help with Post-traumatic stress disorder

- Help with Addictions

- Reduced Worry

- Increased focus

- Better relaxation

- Increased energy

- Feeling happier

Additionally, considering that stress can cause all manner of health problems, by reducing stress, the benefits of meditation can be multiplied many times.

# Types of Meditation

**Meditation focusing on a particular outcome.**
For example, expressing love and kindness to everyone or solving a particular problem.

**Focusing on the Body.**
This includes progressive relaxation and scanning the body.

**Mindfulness Meditation.**
This involves suspending all judgment and focusing on the present rather than the past or the future. Mindfulness is present in most kinds of meditation when for example, you are focusing on your body, your breath or a guided meditation. Mindfulness meditation can also be practiced outside of your daily meditation practice. For example, whilst you are going about your daily activities your mind is focused in the present with all critical thinking and judgment suspendered. More about this later when I explain meditation practice.

**Yoga**
Some forms of yoga combine meditation such as Kundalini which is a physically active form of meditation that combines movements with deep breathing and mantras. You usually need to learn this with a teacher but can subsequently practice at home.

## Contemplation Meditation

Contemplation meditation involves contemplating something. The most common contemplation subject is God as is the case in Raj Yoga.

## Zen Meditation

Zen meditation, sometimes called Zazen is a form of meditation that can be part of Buddhist practice. This is best learnt with a teacher because this kind of meditation involves specific steps and postures. The goal is to find a comfortable position, focus on breathing, and mindfully observe one's thoughts without judgment.

Again, this form of meditation is like mindfulness meditation but requires more discipline and practice. People may be drawn to this type of meditation if they are seeking a spiritual path.

## Transcendental Meditation

Transcendental Meditation is based on the Vedic knowledge which goes back many thousands of years. Vedic Meditation was introduced into the western world as Transcendental Meditation in the 1950's by Mararishi Mahesh Yogi. It was made well known in 1967 when the Beatles learnt meditation with Mararishi. Since then a significant number of celebrities have and are currently practicing Transcendental Meditation and actively recommend it. Transcendental Meditation uses a silent mantra to quieten the mind. This mantra is given by a Transcendental Meditation teacher along with tuition and instructions. Participants practice for two 20-

minute sessions a day.

## Meditation as taught in this book

We are aiming for all the benefits of meditation I have written about previously. Which include reducing stress, eliminating worry and becoming calmer with increasing energy. But as the title of this book suggests, I will be guiding you through specific techniques to help with any mental health issues you need to resolve. Some if not most of these meditation techniques are taken from the different types of meditation. Some are unique for the purpose of helping with a mental health problem or stress. However, this meditation technique is recommended even if you are perfectly fine and just want to achieve a state of continued wellbeing.

I was fortunate in that the first book I ever read on meditation was by the late Barry Long, a well-known meditation guru and spiritual leader of his time. His foundation carries on. Barry wrote that the purpose of meditation was to find the state of stillness within you and after stillness the secret is self-separation. He also said that the purpose of meditation is to get to know yourself... your real self. Now, please don't confuse the state of stillness with being vacant and unaware. Far from it, you are more aware. Imagine a large lion poised, still, silent, and alert ready to pounce on its prey. 100 percent aware. That is the kind of still and aware I am writing about. Look into your pet's eyes, they have no thoughts going through their heads like you do, but; they are very much aware and able to act in an instant.

Self-separation which at first you will experience very briefly in fleeting moments is achieved when you realise that there are two parts of you. The observed and the observer. For example, in meditation when you are silently observing your body, there is the part doing the observing and then there is your body. The aim is to silently observe, your body, breath or whatever you decide to observe or be aware of. This will depend on the type of meditation you are practicing. The aim is to stop the constant internal dialogue of your mind. Starting out, this is very difficult if not impossible. So, we focus the mind for example, on a mantra, on breathing, different parts of the body, guided meditation, or an external object. However, frequently you will find your thoughts come in and off you go on a stream of thoughts. Then again and again you realise this is happening, you stop your thoughts and you go back to your meditation/mantra. This process gets repeated frequently, but each time you notice and stop your thoughts intruding, you gain a degree of self-separation. As you practice you get better at noticing and stopping your thoughts, especially the negative and bad ones! The aim is to make the thoughtless periods longer and longer. Indeed, as you practice these periods do get longer. Persistence is the key thing here!

The aim is to become master of your own mind. The part of your mind we are referring to here is your conscious mind. The part you think is you! Within this part resides mechanical worry, anger, hate, arguing, envy, judging others, fear, regret, and other feelings. Your mind currently controls you and may overwhelm you with negative emotions. So, you see the conscious mind itself is the problem. Therefore, we cannot use the mind to defeat the mind. Therefore, it is important to use the right meditation technique and why some meditation systems fail in this endeavour. The more you meditate using the correct meditation technique which I will show you, the more you will gain control of your mind so negative emotions will begin to go.

Meditation is a lifestyle choice it is an everyday commitment of at least 20 minutes. I say commitment but, it is not a chore, it is a good experience, you will look forward to it and if you miss a day you will feel like you're missing something. That is what people who practice meditation usually say and I can confirm it through personal experience! The best times are in the morning around breakfast time and in the evening around the time after you get home from work or after your evening meal. It does not matter too much, but it is best to get into a regular routine. However, I have found that practicing meditation very close to bedtime when I am tired hinders meditation, as I am fighting off falling asleep and my brain as heading towards the dreaming state.

When you first start out you really should have a daily meditation whether you feel like it all not. But not to worry, you will soon be effortlessly settling down into an easy routine. This is because you are building a new habit. Let me tell you something about habits. It takes approximately 30 days or 4 weeks to get a new habit. So, what happens is that that you focus on doing something for 30 days or so, and then your subconscious mind takes over and you do it automatically. Let me give you an example: imagine that you have a fridge in your kitchen it has been there in the same place for a long time. Then all of a sudden you need to get a new fridge, but it won't fit in the same place, so you have to put your freezer where your fridge was and your fridge where your freezer was. It is a certainty that for the first week you are going to keep going to the freezer without thinking about it when you need milk for your tea or a filling for your sandwich! And so on!

Another example of how we build habits is called for: imagine you go to your dentist and your dentist tells you that you need to start cleaning your teeth in the morning as well as at night. Now, you know some mornings you are going to forget! So, you write a note to yourself on the bathroom mirror which says clean teeth. So, every morning you clean your teeth. Now, imagine after 30 days when it has become a habit and you no longer need a note to remind you, you go back to your dentist and your dentist tells you for some reason, you must stop cleaning your teeth in the morning! When you get home, you will have to write another note to stick on the bathroom mirror which says, "DO NOT CLEAN TEETH"! Otherwise you will clean them without realising you are doing it in the morning without thinking about it!

The next chapter moves on to meditation practice. I have called the meditation in the next chapter Altered State Meditation but, essentially, it is Vedic meditation, based on the ancient Vedic knowledge like Transcendental Meditation. It is the easiest meditation to learn and master, out of all the different meditations, it is the one that requires no concentration or effort and is the easiest to practice. This is, therefore, the meditation that you should start right now and continue to practice as you continue through this book working on your therapy.

Initial Consultation > Journal > Fast Help > Stress Management > Introduction to Meditation > Meditation Practice >

# 7 Meditation Practice

*"Meditation is not a way of making your mind quiet. It's a way of entering into the quiet that's already there – buried under the 50,000 thoughts the average person thinks every day".* Deepak Chopra

## Altered State Meditation

I have called this meditation Altered State Meditation. It is, however, primarily based on Vedic Meditation which uses a mantra to effortlessly calm and still the mind. Vedic meditation comes from the ancient Vedic knowledge going back many thousands of years. No concentration is required and so this is an extremely easy meditation to learn. This means the desired results come much quicker with considerably less effort compared to most other types of meditation.

Vedic meditation is a simple silent natural effortless technique. There is no concentration or control of the mind required. Absolutely no philosophy or religion is involved. There is nothing to believe in and apart from allocating time for your meditation, there is no need for a change in your lifestyle. The technique will even work if you are sceptical.

# THERAPY FOR YOUR MIND

To help explain how it works, it helps to use the analogy similar to the one I used in the previous chapter. The mind is like the ocean. By that, I mean that there are waves on the top and a vast deep, silent calm expanse of water underneath. The waves on the surface of the ocean represent your conscious mind/ego with its thoughts racing along constantly at a fast pace one after the other, often putting a lot of pressure on you. However, the ocean below is vast, large, quiet, and still, just like most of your mind beneath your thoughts. You do not realise this because you currently have little or no access to it.

Vedic meditation is a simple natural effortless technique to help the part of the mind represented by the waves above, to slow down and eventually, to stop for short periods of time. Thus, giving you access to the vast still part of you, the real and larger part of you which I previously labelled as your higher self or superconscious. This whole process involves a deep relaxation which is often deeper than that experienced during sleep. Therefore, stress, anxiety, post-traumatic stress disorder and high blood pressure are considerably alleviated. I have previously mentioned additional benefits in the Introduction to Meditation chapter.

At a minimum, you will need to practice this meditation once a day for 20 minutes. Ideally, you should have two 20-minute sessions a day every day, so this is a lifestyle choice. It is however, worth the rewards both mentally and physically. Ideally, your first meditation should be after you have had breakfast or at least have had some sort of activity and so are wide awake and alert. The second session should be after work or early evening but, not so late that you are getting tired as your bedtime approaches. For most people this may be between 5 and 8pm. You will find that you look forward to your meditation and if you miss it, you really notice it!

## Your mantra

Before you can start your meditation practice, you will need to select your mantra. A great deal has been written about mantras. However, ultimately for our purpose, a mantra is simply a word which when repeated influences the human mind. Whatever mantra you select it should have no meaning to you, otherwise, your mind will latch on to the meaning during your meditation and as it is our aim to still the mind, that is not what you want.

The thinking part of your mind represented by the waves in my analogy above, is naturally and effortlessly drawn and attracted to your mantra. It becomes entrained by it and thus, starts to slow down and initially stops for noticeably short periods of time. These periods get longer with practice. Relaxation is therefore experienced. This technique is different to the difficult concentration and effort methods used by some other meditation techniques.

# Mantra selection

There are a number of different mantra's you could use. For the Vedic meditation you are learning here, it is traditional to use the Vedic Bija or seed mantras. There are around 35 of them in use today. I have chosen four easy to learn and harmonious one's for you. Pick the one which feels right for you:

## Shrim
Pronounced: Shur – ream
shur as when you say shirt and ream as in a quantity of paper or a great amount such as in "*reams* of information".

## Krim
Pronounced: Key-ream
Key as in *key* for a lock and ream as in a quantity of paper or a great amount such as in "*reams* of information".

## Hirim
Pronounced: He – ream
He as in *he* is my brother and ream as in a quantity of paper or a great amount such as in "*reams* of information".

## Shiama
Pronounced: She – arm – a
she as in *she* is my wife, arm as in my hand is attached to my *arm* and a as in, I have *a* cat

# How to use your mantra

After saying your mantra out aloud whilst initially practicing pronouncing it, you should then only repeat your mantra silently in your mind, *not* out aloud. When you are repeating your mantra during your meditation, it is not necessary to keep repeating it in the exact form in which you learnt it. You can certainly aim to start your meditation repeating it in its exact form but, as you progress with your meditation using your mantra, its repetition can end up as only a vague memory of its original form. You may find that you continue again as you originally learnt it as you progress through your meditation and then it fades again into a vague memory. So, feel free to let this happen.

So, you have started your meditation and are now repeating your mantra focusing on how it sounds in your mind. You will find that a thought comes in, initially you will find that a whole train of thoughts come in. When you notice that thoughts have intruded, go back to the mantra and move back to focus on your mantra. You may find that you have thoughts and the mantra both running at the same time. When you notice this, gently favour your mantra over the thought so the thought fades. Do not forcefully try and stop your thoughts. When you notice thoughts, simply move back to the mantra or gently favour the mantra over the thoughts if you notice both are running at the same time.

When repeating your mantra, I want you to notice the

gap in between, by that, I mean I want you to notice the silence in between your mantra each time you repeat it. An ancient Zen observation says that it is the silence between the notes that creates the music. Music without any pauses or silent spaces would be one long note making music impossible. So, notice the beginning and end of your mantra each time you repeat it and the gap in between your repetition of your mantra. When you start your meditation, the gap/silence between each repetition of your mantra maybe barely noticeable. However, as you progress through your meditation you may notice the silence between the repetition of your mantra getting longer as you slow down and relax more into your meditation, until you eventually stop in the gap and silence between your mantra with no thoughts present.

So, as you practice, you may notice that the mantra has stopped, and all thoughts have stopped. Then a thought comes in and so you start the mantra again. This brief period of no thought or mantra is where you have transcended into a higher greatly beneficial state of consciousness. It only needs to last for only seconds for you to get long term benefits. No thoughts and only your mantra is also very beneficial.

*Make sure you memorise this section on how to use your mantra fully in preparation for your meditation.*

# Stress and releasing negative emotions

If you notice any negative or painful emotions, and or stress arising just keep with your mantra and allow the negative emotion/feeling to dissolve in its own time. *Do not* start thinking about the negative feeling. Just notice the feeling as you repeat the mantra. The negative feeling is not the real you, so it will dissolve as you just notice it and repeat the mantra alongside it. Be patient, it will dissolve. If you find thoughts intruding, the same rule applies in that you favour your mantra over the thought.

You will find that stress will naturally be released during your meditation. That is one of the main benefits of this type of meditation. Most of us have a lot of stress and tension to release. A good analogy would be to see stress in the body like a screw that has been turned tighter and tighter. Now in meditation, it is slowly turning the other way and unwinding losing its tension, as it releasees your stress. Think how tight your mussels get under stress and this analogy takes on a reality! That is what a massage does, it releases tension created by stress in your body.

When stress is encountered during meditation prior to release, it can prompt a thought. Not necessary a thought about the stress, but just what seems like a random thought. That means your mantra or thoughtless state is interrupted. You may not be aware that stress has prompted the thought, but that is not important. Just go back to your mantra, or if you are already repeating your mantra, just gently favour your mantra over the thought as I have described above.

# MEDITATION PRACTICE

**The meditation session comprises of 3 parts or modules. Part 1 the relaxation introduction, part 2 the meditation itself which takes up most of the session. Part 3 is the short final part of the session forming the calming and energising visualisation exercise.**

**Before starting:**
Firstly, you need to find a place where you will not be disturbed, and you can sit comfortably. You should be able to sit comfortably in an upright position. Avoid lying down. There is no need to sit in a lotus like position you may have seen in photographs of people meditating. That is how people sit in the eastern countries where the photographs were taken. They find it comfortable sitting that way because that is their normal sitting position. If that is not your normal sitting position, you will find it uncomfortable. If you are uncomfortable it will be difficult for you to meditate. If you find it difficult to find time alone, you may have to get creative like parking somewhere in your car on your way home from work. If practicing at home, just let your family know what you are doing and ask them not to disturb you for 20 minutes. When you get into a routine it will be much easier. So, you have a chair or seat and you have somewhere you

hopefully, will not be disturbed. Make sure you are warm enough.

I would suggest setting a timer for 20 minutes with a tone that is soft and not too startling or loud, especially if you need to be doing something immediately after your meditation. There is a free meditation App you can download on your phone called Insight Timer.

## 1 Relaxation Introduction Module

Before you start your meditation, it is advisable to spend a small amount of time to slowdown and give yourself a bit of space between your daily activities and relax. The following progressive relaxation sequence is easy to remember and practice. Simply start at the top of your body and slowly work down. Just tense and relax each part in sequence from head to toe. It should take no more than two or three minutes

1. Sit upright on your chair with your head erect with your feet a few inches apart.
2. Your hands on your thighs, held loosely together on your lap or resting gently by your side.
3. Look upward slightly and fix your eyes on a spot either real or imaginary in front of you.
4. Tell yourself you are going to silently count to 3 and on the count of 3, your eyes will close, and you will begin to relax.
5. Now count to 3 and let your eyes close.

6. Start your relaxation by fixing your attention on your feet. Begin with your toes, curl your toes, and let them go, notice the sensation as they relax. Let the relaxation rise up into both of your feet. Notice the sensation in your feet.

7. Tense and relax your legs below your knees. Then allow the relaxation to flow up into your calf muscles. Take your time to sense the feeling in your calf muscles.

8. Let the relaxation rise up over your thighs and let both of your legs relax.

9. Now fix your attention on your stomach, relax every muscle, every nerve and every fibre in your stomach as your stomach rests.

10. Now focus on your chest, notice how each deep breath is relaxing you more and more.

11. Now place your attention on your hands and your arms. Begin with your fingers, tightly close your fingers, pause, then open them and feel your hands, relax. Let that relaxation rise up through your hands, wrists, forearms and upper arms. Take your time, notice the physical sensations as your hands, wrists, forearms and upper arms progressively relax.

12. Let that relaxation sweep across your shoulders, notice any areas of tension or tightness in your shoulders, and let it go.

13. Let the relaxation rise up the back of your head, across the top of your head and down to your forehead. Relax your forehead and let any real or imaginary wrinkles go. Now down to your eyes, cheeks, mouth and chin. Let your jaw and whole face relax.

## 2. Mantra Module

Begin using your mantra as described in "**How to use your mantra**" above.

After 20 mins when your timer sounds and/or you have reached the end of your meditation move on to the light visualisation exercise below.

## 3 Light Visualisation Module

This module should only take up a couple of minutes. However, take as long as you need too if you feel anxious or stressed. Sometimes, it is possible that released stress is still awaiting processing at the end of a meditation session.

At the end of your meditation, stop your mantra and visualise a bright round beam of white light mixed with pink and purple heart shapes coming down from the sky/heavens wide enough to surround your whole body.

See your body within this tube of light and see the light moving down into your body from above, through your head and down through your entire body and out through your feet into the Earth below your feet. Notice how this light beam stretches and pulls your feet and legs into the Earth below. See this light continue into the Earth and then back into the sky again, so it forms a complete circle. See your body within this big circle and circuit of white energy. Notice different parts of your body as the light travels down through it. Let your body experience this moving continuous circuit of light and energy. Notice how your body feels.

As you practice, you may notice a warm feeling in

your body as if it was becoming energised. However, be open to all possibilities, there are no right or wrong feelings and its OK if you do not get any at all!

# Start Your meditation session now!

Before proceeding you should have now memorised and practiced your chosen Mantra and have fully memorised and understood the procedures outlined in this chapter up to this point. Remember, you should repeat your mantra silently in your mind, *not* out aloud

Ok, so you are now sitting somewhere with a comfortable temperature. You are comfortable and you will not be disturbed. You have set your timer and you are good to start meditating! After your sessions regularly review the instructions again in this chapter considering your ongoing experience.

I go into the spiritual side of meditation and the associated benefits in the last chapter of this book.

## Simple summary:

1. Select and practice your mantra
2. Sit upright comfortably in a place where you will not be disturbed for 20 minutes
3. Close your eyes and, focus on your feet then progressively relax your body from your feet to the top of your head.
4. Start your mantra and perhaps, subtly noticing the gaps/space between each repetition
5. When thoughts intrude, gently favour your mantra

**Therapy Journal Exercise 3**

Write in your journal how you found the above meditation and keep a record of your experiences with this technique.

If you are new to meditation you will undoubtedly experience a lot of intruding thoughts during your meditation. So, for help with this, now go to the next chapter and practice the techniques described as you continue to practice your meditation for at least one 20-minute session a day, preferably two sessions a day.

Some of the techniques to control your thoughts in the next chapter can be used outside of your meditation sessions in the course of your everyday life.

**Initial Consultation > Journal > Fast Help > Stress Management > Introduction to Meditation > Meditation Practice > Thought and Emotion Control >**

*Whilst the above meditation requires considerably less effort than mindfulness meditation, I have included a mindfulness meditation in the Appendix.*

# 8. Thought & Emotion Control

*"Knowing Yourself - The true in the false, gradually strips away all self-delusion until all that remains is pure being."* Barry Long

## Your internal thought dialogues

Your thoughts and internal dialogue can be helpful in solving life's problems, navigating you through everyday life and working out solutions. However, you will have noticed that often your thoughts runaway out of your control. These thoughts at best are non-productive and often negative. This involves worry, fear about the future, persistently reviewing events and making up future scenarios. Often these thoughts produce a wave of emotion and then the negative thoughts get carried on this wave of negative emotion. This makes an overwhelming combination.

By practicing the Vedic meditation in the previous chapter, you will start to gain control over your thoughts. However, as you continue with your meditation practice, I need to explain more about intruding thoughts, there is going to be a lot of them as you start to train your mind. Your aim is to stop your internal thought dialogue, to quieten your mind. Your aim is to just observe whatever you are focusing on whether it is your body, mantra, your breath or a visualisation. Absolutely no thinking about what you are focusing on or analytically thinking about what you are experiencing or doing.

But despite your best efforts you will find your mind running off on a train of thoughts. Then, you will realise what is happening and return back to your meditation. You may be inclined to get frustrated. But please do not! if you do it will only make your meditation more difficult. Instead you should know that each time you realise you have run off on a stream of thoughts and stop and return to your meditation, you are gaining more control of your mind. It may be only for short periods to start with but, it will gradually get longer. Anything that can be made to obey for a few seconds can be made to obey forever. When your mind is still without any thoughts, your higher self is the quite observer.

Each time you notice thoughts intruding, you gain a degree of self-separation. There is the part of you that suddenly realised and noticed the thoughts and stopped them. Like the deep ocean noticing the waves (thoughts) on its surface in my previous analogy of the mind. There are therefore, two parts of you, the part that stopped the thoughts is the deep powerful silent part of you.

To help you gain control of intruding thoughts, when you notice that a thought has intruded into your meditation, try this technique: freeze the intruding thought in your mind's eye and then trace your thoughts back by linking and connecting backwards to where the first one intruded into your meditation. Sometimes you get side-tracked and have to start again. But that is how it is as you practice. Another way of describing this technique is by using a movie/film example: when you realise your mind has run off on a train of thoughts, see that train of thoughts as a movie or length of film made up of individual sections or scenes. Each section or scene represents a thought. Each section/thought is logically linked together and runs forward like a movie.

## The Pause Button

When you finally realise you are thinking again whilst you should be meditating. Visualise the symbol representing a pause button of the type found on your remote control that pauses a film consisting of a symbol of two parallel lines. Then place the imaginary pause button over the image of the thought in your mind with the intention of pausing and freezing that thought in its tracks. Effectively leaving you with a still image in your mind, just like you get if you paused a film on your computer, phone or television screen.

When you have frozen the thought, imagine pressing an imaginary rewind button to review all the previous thoughts linked to it. So, you are effectively rewinding the film of your previous thoughts in your mind backwards reviewing each thought in turn until you get back to where you left your meditation. Then return to your meditation. Sometimes you may lose your way, but this is a great way for gaining control over your thoughts and getting better at meditating. Practice and persistence are the key.

A powerful variation of the above technique is to pause and freeze your thought by visualising a pause button over it as described above. Then see the frozen thought in 3 dimensions (3D) observe it from different angles, notice that it is not part of you, notice that the thought is not real and therefore it is a false part of you, which the real part of you can control. You have just experienced self-separation. Keep practicing!

It is very important not to get annoyed with yourself when you discover a thought intruding. I will say it again! It is very important *not* to get annoyed with yourself when you discover a thought intruding. If you do, your conscious mind is criticising itself, you feel bad and it will be detrimental to your meditation. So just observe that you have stopped a train of thoughts again and go back to your meditation. You could visualise the pause button described above and rewind your thoughts as above. Then continue with your meditation. At other times, just stop your thoughts and return to your mantra or visualisation exercise.

*Set a timer if you need to return to everyday life at a particular time.*

# Active meditation during your normal day

When you start to practice meditation, you are attempting to train your mind by controlling your thoughts. This means that you are gaining the ability to stop your thinking or train of thoughts should you wish to do so. You are practicing this during meditation because meditation is about quietening your mind. But you can also practice stopping your thoughts during your normal daily activities. This will not only help you become fully proficient at meditation quicker. It will also give you more control over your thoughts in your daily life. This will become invaluable in the future if you find yourself in an emotionally charged state with runaway worrying thoughts. However, even in its normal state of operation, your mind can and does, run off on a train of thoughts you would rather not be thinking. For these reasons you will find the practice of active meditation very valuable and the good thing is, it won't take up any more of your time!

You will effectively be practicing self-separation because you will be observing from a mentally quite but nevertheless alert state. Notice how an animal (such as your pet) can do this. The part of you that is doing the observing is your high self. It works at a higher level where thoughts are not required. It is a state of instant knowing. You could compare it to analogue and digital in electrical terms. Thoughts are equivalent to the slow less powerful analogue device and your high self to the faster and more powerful digital device.

# Exercises:

## Adverts _listening_

When listing to a commercial radio station focus on
only hearing the words. Suspend all mental dialogue.
Do not analyse what is being said. Do not judge what
is being said. Have no thoughts. Just hear the sound
with your internal dialogue suspended and frozen.
Just focus on what is being said. Observe only, listen
with a silent mind. No opinions or judgments.

Do the same with a visual and audio advert on
television for example.

## In conversations

When engaged in conversations, observe your
reaction to what is being said. What assumption are
you making?
On hearing strangers talking in public places.
Observe your curiosity, see yourself getting imaginary
involved in other people's events. Then stop your
thoughts and just hear their words. Listen with
silence.

## Judgments

When thinking about someone, notice your judgments
about that person. Observe your self making that
judgment. It is your false self making that judgment.
your higher self does not judge.

## Exercise when walking

Observe the movement of your legs and arms, keep
your head level and observe your surroundings
seeing how it changes as you walk. You could pick

just one aspect of your surroundings such as the trees, grass, or pavement. Observe only, no internal dialogue, no thinking, no opinions, no judgements.

**Meditate in idle moments**
On the train or bus or in bed for example.

**Meditation on removing negative feelings & emotions as they arise**

In this exercise, instead of observing your body as in a progressive relaxation, you are going to be observing your negative feelings and emotions. This can also be done outside of your usual meditation session in a wide-awake state whenever you can stop your daily activity for 5 minutes.

You do this exercise by just observing your emotion. In this way the emotion, the false part of you, will dissolve. The false part dies. When the false part dies it is like being a heart broken lover who now discovers they are now free of feeling for their former lover.

So, when you notice you have a negative emotion or feeling, stop your thoughts and just observe the emotion with no thoughts until the emotion dissolves. Persist just observing until the emotion or negative feeling finally disappears.

So, notice where in your body you have the feeling you want to remove. Focus on it silently, do *not* think about it, just notice how it feels as you focus on the feeling without analysis and without judgment. Do not think, just feel and just observe. You must remain the uninvolved observer so no analysis, no reason, do not condemn. Do not try to change anything, just observe. No thinking or internal dialogue.

As you persist in this way, you will notice the bad feeling starts to disappear and then as you continue to persist as I have indicated above, the bad/negative feeling will disappear completely. Make sure you persist until the feeling subsides, it will, but you must persist with no thoughts, just observe.

You are practicing self-separation; your higher self is the observer and your negative emotion or feeling is the observed. The observed is the false in you, it's not a natural part of you, it wasn't with you when you were born. As the real higher you, observes the false you, the false will get disregarded just as you would disregard anything you discovered was false in your daily life.

Up until now, you have experienced your negative feelings and simultaneously thought about them whilst you were experiencing them. This has meant you were using the false part of you, the ego/personality that houses those negative feelings to observe itself. That means that the negative emotion or feeling stays with you longer and returns often. When you observe your negative or bad feeling in mental silence it is your true and higher self doing the observing *not* your ego/personality, so the false gets dissolved, and therefore is less likely to return.

84

# THERAPY FOR YOUR MIND

Noble Prize winner Doctor David R. Hawkins, MD., Ph.D. in his book "Power Vs. Force, The Hidden Detriments of Human Behaviour", writes: that from an early age that he experienced profound deep states of meditation and wrote *"... I discovered that I could perceive the reality that underlay personalities; I saw how the origin of emotional sickness lay in people's belief that they were their personalities. And so, of its own, my practice resumed and eventually became huge..."*.

If the feeling does return it may originate from a different part of you. The important thing is that you keep repeating the meditation process I have described above each time a negative emotion or feeling arises and persist with it. And remember you can do this exercise in your full daily active waking state outside of your dedicated meditation practice.

To help with the above exercise, you can use and adapt the "Pause Button Technique" I have described earlier in this chapter. Here it is again: Whilst you are attempting to stop your thoughts and just focus on your feeling or emotion, first visualise the symbol representing a pause button of the type found on your remote control, that pauses a film consisting of two parallel lines. Then place it over the image of the thought in your mind with the intention of pausing and freezing the thought in its tracks. Effectively leaving you with a still image, just like you get if you paused a film on your computer, phone or television screen. This is an effective way of stopping your train of thought, as without movement thoughts will cease and lose their power.

Additionally, to help further, whilst attempting to silently observe your emotion or feeling with no thoughts, you could keep repeating your mantra as you used previously in the Vedic / altered state meditation technique in the previous chapter.

Napoleon Hill said, *"Persistence in man is what carbon is to steel"*. What he meant was, if you persist with something, you can and will achieve whatever you set your mind upon. Your persistence is as strong as carbon cutting through steel.

I will finish this last meditation chapter with two quotes:

*"The purpose of meditation is to transcend the mind and its mental activities and limited perceptions, thereby transcending duality and becoming increasingly aware of Oneness"*.

Doctor David R. Hawkins, MD., Ph.D.


*"Then in observing your feelings, emotions, habits (the false) your higher self is doing the observing and so is the observer. By being the still detached observer of the observed you are separating yourself out"*.

Barry Long

## Therapy Journal exercise 4

Keep a record of your progress and have a meditation session at least once a day. Mark each day you meditate on your calendar, diary, or journal. It is particularly important you have a daily meditation session.

Do not forget to practice controlling your thoughts outside of your meditation sessions as described in this chapter.

Read the Spiritual Approach chapter to gain a deeper understanding of meditation

Read the Personal Development chapter before you start on the Memory & Emotion Recall Therapy chapter and set your goals.

**Initial Consultation > Journal > Fast Help > Stress Management > Introduction to Meditation > Meditation Practice > Thought & Emotion Control > Spiritual Part >**

# 9. Memory & Emotion Recall Therapy

*"The conscious mind may be compared to a fountain playing in the sun and falling back into the great subterranean pool of subconscious from which it rises".*

Sigmund Freud

**Before reading this chapter, re-read the Initial Consultation chapter to refresh your memory.**

**Have your journal with you before starting this chapter.**

This chapter involves detailed work with your memory. Emotions get locked into some memories, normally the painful ones. Often these memories can then become difficult to retrieve and so the emotions stay locked away causing problems. This process was described in detail in the Initial Consultation chapter. I have just explained it in a slightly different way here. This was known in ancient times. The Toltecs in what is now Mexico had a therapy using memory retrieval which they called Recapitulation. It was basically a technique to retrieve and review memories. Which in turn released repressed and hidden feelings and emotions which were causing the types of negative symptoms of the type I have described in the Initial C onsultation chapter. Anthropologists such as Carlos Castaneda and Victor Sanchez have documented these recapitulation techniques.

The function of recapitulation according to the ancient Toltec civilisation is summed up beautifully by anthropologist Victor Sanchez.

*"Recapitulation is the natural process of energetic restoration of our energetic body from the damages that come from the past. This natural act is done by the body. It consists of bodily remembering and reliving the meaningful events in our lives in order to perform a healing process to recover the state of energetic completeness that we had when we were born".*

More recently, Freud used a similar concept in his psychoanalysis methods. However, for the best results it is best to use memory recall with a slight change in one's level of consciousness. Different states of consciousness are associated with different brain frequencies.

We can determine your brains frequency by hooking it up to an EEG monitor of the type found in a hospital. Different frequencies are associated with different levels of consciousness.

The wide-awake state Beta state gives a brain frequency of 12 to 38 cycles per second (hertz).

The Alpha state in which we are very relaxed and possibly daydreaming, gives a brain frequency of between 8 to 12 cycles per second.

The theta state on which you will be in a deep meditative state has a brain frequency of 3 to 8 cycles per second.

The Delta state has a brain frequency of 0.5 to 3 cycles per second and is a dreamless state.

It has been found that a relaxed state of consciousness associated with the alpha state (such as that used in hypnotherapy) considerably helps with memory recall therapy of the type associated with the ancient recapitulation method and the more recent psychoanalysis therapies.

This module/chapter runs alongside your regular daily meditation program and uses your journal and a one hour a week dedicated meditation type session. There are two parts to it, journal work and the dedicated meditation type session. Just doing the journal part without the dedicated 1-hour altered state meditation type session would still give you benefits but the two parts together are considerably more effective. You will however need to persevere. Once you start however, the healing and memory recall process takes on a life of its own. It's like starting a ball rolling down a hill, the healing and memory recall process keeps going between sessions.

Because the process involves retrieving memories from the past you may sometimes also notice emotions accompanying those memories, all manner of different emotions and feelings, this naturally means that some will be unpleasant. But that's good, because those negative feelings and emotions were producing negative symptoms! And when those negative emotions are released it is like letting a mad rabid dog out of a cage, there is no way you can get it back in again! That particular negative emotion is gone for good.

You start the Journal part first because it provides a start and basis for the 1-hour altered state meditation type session. This is a substitute for an analytical hypnotherapy session normally used in person with a hypnotherapist. It is based on the free association technique pioneered by Freud but enhanced by the altered alpha conscious state which in this context could be called self-hypnosis. This technique was used extensively by the International Association of Hypnotherapists (IAH) started in the 1970's by Neil French. I was a member of this Association and at one time had three separate clinics helping numerous patients with this method.

Ideally, a one to one consultation with a qualified therapist works best with one session a week usually a minimum of 8. But often many more depending on the severity of the symptoms and how responsive the patient is. This however is dependent on finding a therapist and being able to afford the ongoing session fee which can be prohibitive if multiple weekly sessions are required. This is what happened to me back in 1985. After a very traumatic childhood I suffered from an anxiety and depression that made it very difficult to talk and interact with people. I had researched and learnt self-hypnosis from books and by luck, living in remote Wales, I managed to find a hypnotherapist specialising in analytical hypnotherapy. I had two sessions which helped immensely in releasing painful emotions. However, it was clear that I would need more sessions.

The only problem was that there was no way I could afford to pay for anymore. I was young and on a low wage at that time. Luckily, I managed to purchase a book published in 1984 by Neil French called "Successful hypnotherapy, An Investigation of Mankind Under the Microscope of Hypnosis". This gave more details on the analytical free association method. This involved weekly sessions with a suitably qualified therapist. Back to square one, I could not afford to see a suitably qualified therapist!

They say necessity is the mother of all invention. Well, I adapted the free association analysis technique using self-hypnosis, a similar if not the same state experienced in some meditations. I found that anxiety and tension was released in almost all of my sessions. I gave myself two sessions a week and

6 months later, I was feeling considerably better and able to interact and talk with people due to a lack of anxiety. Many years later I went on to train with the IAH and Neil French and qualified in 1998. Subsequently, I have taken many patients successfully through the process. Which at one time involved working from 3 separate clinics.

If I were to put it into my own words to illustrate the goal of this chapter/module, I would say that my aim would be to get you back to the state that you were in before fate intervened. So, let us get started.

Stage one is journal work where basically; you write down a list summarising with just a heading, your life history in a structured manner. This has three purposes:

1. To serve as a starting point for each therapy session if needed and to provide a structure for therapy if needed. This includes sessions with a therapist if you wish.
2. To help recover hidden memories and their linked associated emotions
3. To function as a practical therapeutic journaling tool in its own right.

So, let us get started with this section of your journal. I recommend putting time aside to write your list in your journal. Ideally an hour each time. Also work at your list regularly to avoid losing the momentum of recall from the previous session.

# Journal work part 1

Under the following headings write a list of people as it applies to you. Just write what comes to mind. You can take your time and revisit the list many times. So, do not stop because you are having difficulty remembering at any time. You will find more names come each time you go back to writing the list.

- Relatives

- Friends

- Partners

- People you knew at school

- Work mates

- People related to your hobby or interest

- Any significant persons not included above

- Now if applicable, write a list of significant events that you experienced whilst being alone.

# Journal work part 2

Now write down a list of significant events that occurred whilst you have lived with each person. Do not describe the event in detail, just a limited number of words just sufficient to remind you of that event. Now, If applicable; write a list of significant events experienced whilst you were alone.

For now, it is important **not** to start analysing the event, just observe and list it.

Each list could start in a chronological order if you find that helps. By that I mean from the last or from the first time you met them to the last time of contact, but it is not necessary to do it this way. You will find that each time you go back to working on your list you will remember additional events. Most likely, you will have memories coming back in between writing the list in your journal. So, write them down wherever you are so you can enter them into your journal later.

## Therapy sessions

When you have finished or have listed a reasonable amount of memories in your journal, you can move on to your 1-hour altered state meditation type session. Let us call them your therapy sessions.

They work in a similar way to your meditation sessions but last longer. Usually, up to an hour. There are three separate parts to the session.

1. Relaxation module
2. Free association exercise
3. Session closing procedure

*See the appendix for details of audio guides.*

## Relaxation Module

This is the same as the relaxation module from the altered state meditation which you have been practicing. I have reprinted it below. You need to be able to sit or lay down somewhere comfortable where you will not be disturbed for the next hour. You can set a timer that is not to startling if you have commitments immediately after your session. You can however add a short bit onto the end as you will see below.

Before you start, it is advisable to spend a small amount of time to slowdown and give yourself a bit of space between your daily activities and relax. The following progressive relaxation sequence is easy to remember and practice. Simply start at the top of your body and slowly work down. Just tense and relax each part in sequence from head to toe. It should take approximately five minutes.

1. Sit upright on your chair with your head erect with your feet a few inches apart.
2. Your hands on your thighs, held loosely together on your lap or resting gently by your side.
3. Look upward slightly and fix your eyes on a spot either real or imaginary in front of you.
4. Tell yourself you are going to silently count to 3 and on the count of 3, your eyes will close, and you will begin to relax.
5. Now count slowly to 3 and let your eyes close on the count of 3.
6. Start your relaxation by fixing your attention on your feet. Begin with your toes, curl your toes, and let them go, notice the sensation as they relax. Let the relaxation rise up into

both of your feet. Notice the sensation in your feet.

7. Tense and relax your legs below your knees. Then allow the relaxation to flow up into your calf muscles. Take your time to sense the feeling in your calf muscles.

8. Let the relaxation rise up over your thighs and let both of your legs relax.

9. Now fix your attention on your stomach, relax every muscle, every nerve and every fibre in your stomach as your stomach rests.

10. Now focus on your chest, notice how each deep breath is relaxing you more and more.

11. Now place your attention on your hands and your arms. Begin with your fingers, tightly close your fingers, pause, then open them and feel your hands, relax. Let that relaxation rise up through your hands, wrists, forearms and upper arms. Take your time, notice the physical sensations as your hands, wrists, forearms and upper arms progressively relax.

12. Let that relaxation sweep across your shoulders, notice any areas of tension or tightness in your shoulders, and let it go.

13. Let the relaxation rise up the back of your head, across the top of your head and down to your forehead. Relax your forehead and let any real or imaginary wrinkles go. Now down to your eyes, cheeks, mouth and chin. Let your jaw and whole face relax.

**Additional add-on to relaxation module**

Imagine standing at the top of a flight of steps or stairs, each step is numbered from 1 to 10. Tell yourself that each step you take down will take you down to deeper levels of relaxation and when you get to the bottom you will be as relaxed as you can ever be. Now count slowly from 1 to 10 telling yourself your relaxing further and further with each step that you take.

# Free Association Module

Free association works by linking one memory to another without judgment or analytical thought. One memory just links to another memory just like parts of a conversation naturally flow from one topic to another. I will explain further by using an analogy. Imagine a large long chain made up of its separate links. Each separate link represents a memory. As you get to one link it automatically links to another. If you look down the length of the long chain, you will see all memories are ultimately linked to each other. This is the same within your subconscious mind. Some of those memories will be hidden down the chain, some of these hidden memories will have painful emotions attached which will be causing negative symptoms. By recalling the memories before this problematic memory, you will get to the one causing the problem and automatically release the emotion attached to it which was having a negative affect on you.

It is absolutely vital that you don't analyse what you

are remembering, you just want a running commentary of the recollection or memory. This is the right way for example:

"I am riding down the street on my bike and I am getting wet because it's raining".

The following is intellectualising and *not* what we want:

"I am riding down the street on my bike and I am getting wet because it is raining. *Now when did I get that bike? I wonder which birthday it was.*

So, we just want a running commentary of your memory. Unless you are with your therapist there is no need to speak out aloud.

You can start the session using a memory from your journal if one does not arise. Likewise, you can take another memory from your journal if your memories come to a halt during the session. So, I would suggest taking time to quickly review your journal before starting the free association module, so you do not need to refer to it during the free association part of your session.

If any painful memories arise take some slow deep breaths until the feeling goes. You can also use the Emo Trance method from the fast guide chapter to release any tensions or bad feelings as they arise. So, make sure you practice this beforehand, so you understand the procedure. You can also cut a session short if you are struggling with bad feelings and spend

20 mins in meditation to calm down and relax.

## Closing the session

When your hour is up, and your timer sounds or before that if you have had enough, it is time to close the session. Sometimes you may just feel that it is enough so then it is OK to stop. When I was doing it on my own, I would feel that my head was full and just knew it was time to end the session. Anyway, when you are ready to end the session. I would suggest taking a few deep breaths and just letting your mind drift to a peaceful place and relax there for a few minutes. Then tell yourself that you are going to count backwards from 3 to 1 and that on the count of 1 you will open your eyes and be wide awake.

## After your session

In your journal now write a summary of what you have remembered together with any emotions or feelings experienced. Remember to date your entry. That is it until your next weekly session! If you find memories surfacing in-between sessions which is highly likely, write them down in your journal. Also, write your dreams in your journal if they are notable.

# 10. Stress Management

*"Stress is not what happens to us. It's our response to what happens. And response is something we can choose".* Maureen Killoran

## Introduction

### The Stress Test
How stressed are you? Open your journal on a new blank page in readiness for the stress test below:

Because everyone reacts to stress in their own way, no one stress test can give you a complete diagnosis of your stress levels. This stress test is intended to give you an overview only. It is not intended as a substitute for professional medical or psychological care. If in doubt, always consult your doctor.

Please write the list below in your journal and write "yes" or "no" next to each statement as it applies to you. Answer yes, even if only part of a question applies to you. Take your time, but please be totally honest with your answers:

1. I frequently work at home at night, on work which I have brought home

2. I feel that there are just not enough hours in the working day to do all of the things that I must do

3. I can frequently feel impatient with the speed at which events take place

4. At times I can have an extreme reluctance to go to work

5. I try to fit more and more tasks into less and less time, resulting in me not allowing time for any unforeseen problems that may arise

6. I feel that there are too many deadlines in my work / life that are difficult to meet

7. My self-confidence / self-esteem is low

8. I can frequently have a vaguely guilty feeling if I relax and do nothing, even for short periods of time

9. I find myself thinking about problems to do with my personal / business / professional life, even when I am supposed to be engaged in recreational pursuits

10. I can have a feeling of intense fatigue, even when I wake after sleep

11. I can / do find myself finishing other people's sentences for them

12. I have a tendency to eat, talk, move and walk

quickly

13. My appetite has altered, either to a desire to go on a binge, especially on sweet, sugary foods, or I have suffered a loss of appetite

14. I find myself becoming irritated / angry if the car or traffic in front of me seems to me to be going too slowly / I become very frustrated at having to wait in a queue

15. I can feel anger and resentment at nothing in particular and/or I have a feeling that something is missing, but I don't know what

16. I'm aware that I try to get other people to hurry up / get on with it

17. At times I feel depressed, tearful, irritable, all-over tension, short tempered, unusual clumsiness, concentration / memory is impaired, excessive perspiration

18. I find that if I have to do repetitive tasks, I become impatient

19. I can seem to be listening to other people's conversation, even though I am in fact preoccupied with my own thoughts

20. My sex drive is lower, or I feel sexually unsatisfied

21. I find myself grinding my teeth, especially if I am stressed or feeling impatient

22. I seem to have an increase in aches and pains, especially in the neck, head, jaw, lower back, shoulders, chest. For women: Menstrual cycles are erratic, often missed

23. At times I am unable to perform work or tasks as well as I used to, or I feel my judgement is clouded / not as good as it was

24. I find I have a greater dependency on alcohol, caffeine, nicotine or drugs (whether prescription or not)

25. I find that I do not have time for many interests / hobbies outside of work

A **yes** answer scores **1** (one), and a **no** answer scores **0** (zero).

Now, total up all your **yes** scores.
If you score:

**4 points or less:** You have no need to worry about being prone to stress. You are least likely to suffer from stress-related illness. You are also the least likely to have a stress-related heart attack.

**5 - 13 points:** You are prone to stress. You are also more likely to suffer from the negative effects of stress. You may possibly be open to stress-related illness. You are in need of stress control management / counselling.

**14 points or more:** You are the most prone to the negative effects of stress. You are more open to stress-related illness and possible heart attack. You must do something about it. I would advise that you seek professional stress management counselling and consult your doctor.

OK, let us see how you can deal with and reduce your stress:

The word stress can be defined in different ways. However, for the purpose of this Stress Management chapter I will define stress as "the emotional, physiological and psychological effects caused by a build-up of either internally or externally generated mental pressure".

The last thing that most people who are suffering from excessive stress will admit to is the fact that they are suffering from the effects of stress, or that they cannot handle that stress. They tend to view it as some sort of weakness to even admit to having excessive stress in their lives. It can seem like a weakness to admit to family, friends and work colleagues that they are under too much pressure. They can be afraid that their employer will see it as a sign of weakness, and / or a sign that they cannot do their job properly. This puts extra worry and stress on the nervous system, making an already poor situation appear to be even more intolerable.

However, when someone is living a life full of stress, it becomes their normal life, and it becomes difficult to compare how they would feel if they were not stressed. Therefore, it becomes easy to live a life full of the effects of stress and not realise that you are stressed. This is because it has become your new normal for you. However, there is no getting away from the effects of stress. Stress can arise from deep-seated unresolved emotional conflicts stored at a subconscious level or from your life's current situations. It can of course be a mixture of both. However, for the purpose of this chapter I will be dealing with stress likely to come from life's current situations. However, the techniques for dealing with stress in this chapter should help regardless as to where it comes from.

The aim of this chapter is to enable you to recognise the effect that excessive stress can have upon your mind and body. And, put you in control of your own mind and body, enabling you to learn to manage the negative effects of stress, to cope with stressful situations that may arise in your life, whether they be a dramatic event, or just the everyday act of getting on with work and living life, so that you can enjoy life. What you will *not* be doing, is taking away all stress from your life.

Stress can come in many guises. It can be caused by many different things. Stress will manifest itself in a myriad of ways, but remember, we all need an amount of stress in our lives, to be able to survive, to be able to do our jobs, and to give us the will and the energy to cope with emergencies. Stress is not only helpful and necessary; it can often be a positive force in your life. When you have a deeper understanding of stress and its negative effects on you, you will actually find that you can learn to control the negative psychological and physical affects that it has upon you. This control over yourself will enable you to use stress to work for you, not against you.

Stress can and does affect men and women from all walks of life, young and old, rich, and poor, no matter what your job, or even if you have no job. Stress and its affects have no respect for your status or position, or lack of it, in life.

Most emotional stress is about what may happen, "what if this happens, what if that happens?" It has nothing to do with the here and now. Emotional stress is about what we think may occur in the future. In a word, we anticipate some sort of threat to our well-being. This feeling, that something of a threatening nature will occur, is the primary factor in causing most of the stress conditions that have such an adverse effect on our lives.

In this chapter you will find general information on stress and its effects on the mind and body. Along with the advice in this chapter, you should be using a relaxation technique. Ideally, it will consist of a minimum of twenty minutes of meditation each day. However, I have recorded a free specific dedicated guided relaxation program to use with this chapter. Please see the Appendix for details. Please read through all this chapter before using the audio.

You can play the relaxation program audio at any time of the day, but you may find that if you play it last thing at night, just before bedtime, you will find that it will help you to go to sleep. Most people will listen to the relaxation audio two or three times feeling wide awake, after this you will more than likely appear to fall asleep whilst listening. This does not matter, as your subconscious mind is still wide awake, even when you close your eyes, and you will not, at any time, lose control of your senses.

You will be fully aware, at all times, of everything that is going on around you, it just will not bother you. However, if there is an emergency, if someone knocks on your door, or calls your name, or if the telephone rings, you will open your eyes and deal with the interruption without any feelings of lethargy or tiredness getting in the way.

# Audio Relaxation Program

### Step One
You will require about 35 minutes a day in which you will not be disturbed. You can sit in a comfortable chair or, better still, lie on your bed. Don't cross your arms or legs. You may find it beneficial to use headphones whilst listening to the relaxation program, although it can be used successfully without.

The effects of the positive suggestions contained in the relaxation audio are cumulative. This means that the process of stress control starts immediately, but, because each of us is an individual, the full benefits of the program may take a few weeks to build up and to be felt in full.

**Step Two**

You will obtain maximum benefit from the relaxation program if you play the audio once a day for at least two weeks. This will stimulate your unconscious mind in being more alert, wider awake, more energetic, resulting in you being more confident in yourself and your own abilities. Thus, enabling you to control and to handle the negative effects of any stressful situations that may arise in your life. Although it is to your benefit to listen to the program on a daily basis, it will not matter much if you miss an occasional day, it will just take that little bit longer before you gain the maximum benefit from the program.

You only need to play the relaxation audio program once a day, but if you feel that you will benefit from occasionally playing the audio program more than once a day, this will do you no harm. You cannot overdose on the relaxation program. If, at any time in the future, you feel that you need a boost, all you need to do is to play the relaxation program once a day for a week.

*If you are in any doubt about your condition, always consult your doctor. Warning - Never play the audio relaxation program whilst driving or operating machinery.*

## The Calm Technique

The Calm Technique which I have written about in the fast help chapter is a relaxation technique that you can use for fighting back against stress. It is especially good for fighting against the after effects of stress, and you will soon find that you can become much more relaxed and calmer, in no more than a minute. You can do this at any time of the day or night.

The Calm Technique is a powerful technique which may be used in any situation that you feel is stressful or is about to become stressful. You can also use this technique anywhere, in a crowded room, or in front of another person. No one will ever know you are doing it.

During the course of your day check your breathing regularly. Get into the habit of monitoring your breathing in a variety of situations, such as: first thing in the morning upon waking, during and after being stuck in congested traffic, during a meal break, prior to an important meeting, perhaps with the boss, or a client, even after an argument with your spouse or partner. In fact, check your breathing at any time that you think you are stressed, or about to become stressed.

You will find that with practice you will soon learn that

you can calm and relax yourself mentally and physically in less than 60 seconds, just by following the simple steps outlined below:

1. Breathe in through the nose, and out through the mouth.

2. Become aware of your breathing, breathe slowly and deeply. Feel your stomach muscles slowly starting to relax.

3. Take a deep breath, at the same time pulling in your stomach muscles.

4. Hold this breath for a mental count of 3. As you slowly expel the air through your mouth, say silently to yourself the word **"Calm"**.

5. Repeat this twice more, again saying silently the word **"Calm"** as you exhale. When you've taken those 3 deep breaths, just allow the word **"Calm"** to drift around in your mind

You will, with regular checking of the way you are breathing, find out how different situations affect your breathing patterns. If you find that you are predominantly taking quick, shallow breaths, get yourself into the habit of breathing more slowly and deeply. This will have the effect of reducing the risk of you hyperventilating.

Slow, deep breathing, using your diaphragm, uses all of your lungs. By using your full lung capacity, you get the air to the lower parts of the lungs, which are the richest in blood vessels, enabling the process of expansion and ventilation to occur more efficiently. During stressful or perceived stressful situations, slow, deep breathing will also have the effect of calming you and making you more composed. It will help with relaxation and will also reduce those feelings of tension and helplessness. It will give you a much greater sense of control over your own emotions, your own body, and your own mind.

Remember, in times of stress to take those 3 very deep breaths and use that word **"Calm"**. Monitor your breathing regularly. Breathe deeply and slowly.

## Stress and its effects

Prolonged excessive stress can lead to depression. Both depression and stress can affect the immune system. This in turn opens you up to certain physical illnesses such as the high risk of a heart attack.

At times of stress or perceived stress, our adrenal glands, which are located above the kidneys, release into the bloodstream the hormones Adrenaline, Noradrenaline and Cortisol.

These hormones, which are also produced by nerve cells, are immensely powerful, stimulating chemicals, which affect almost every organ in our body, including the intestines, appendix, eyes, bladder and tonsils. These hormones also switch off most metabolic activities, such as the digestive and reproductive systems, which are not needed at times of danger or perceived danger.

The release of these stimulating chemicals into the bloodstream is essential to us. In times of danger they give us the extra energy to help us to run away or stay and fight. (fight or flight). Unfortunately, in this day and age we generally have nowhere to run to nor do we have the opportunity to fight the danger, even if we could see or understand what it is that is threatening us. Because of this we have generated a new response to danger, we freeze, both mentally and physically. Now we have fight, flight or freeze.

Some of the first signs of the onset of stress on the body include alert breathing rhythms, quickening heart rate, raised blood pressure, nerve activation, muscle tension and release of essential body nutrients. These are all designed to give the body the power to cope with danger, or perceived danger.

When we go into freeze mode, our body finds it difficult to dissipate the excessive build-up of adrenaline etc. If we do not dissipate these hormones and their affects from our system, our ability to produce the vital defence substances known as Interferons is drastically reduced. Interferons are antiviral proteins produced by cells that have been invaded by viruses. Cells that are under attack from viruses' release Interferons to provide protection for other cells that may be open to attack from the invading viruses. They also provide protection against any other organism that tries to invade the body. So, if we experience prolonged or excessive stress, not only is our body under direct attack from within, it is also far less able to defend itself from even simple external infections such as the common cold. This makes it harder for your body to cope with a wide range of illnesses. The body and mind become more vulnerable to further stress, our general health declines, and we can enter a vicious downward spiral. This can give rise to negative attitudes and actions.

**Some of the numerous negative effects of Stress:**
- Minor health problems, such as upset stomach, headache, colds, flu, back pain, and muscle pain.

- Cramps and missed menstrual periods can increase. (Caused by too much Cortisol).

- Skin rashes can appear. If you suffer from a skin complaint, such as psoriasis, it can become aggravated.

- One can suffer a loss of confidence, a loss of enthusiasm, and can gain a feeling of low self-esteem, a feeling of hopelessness and depression can set in.

- A feeling of intense fatigue can follow you about all day. Even when you wake

- After sleep, you still feel fatigued and tired.

This is caused by too much Adrenaline.

- Sleep patterns can become distorted, you may find it difficult to go to sleep, then waking at 3 or 4 A.M.

- Indigestion and eating disorders.

- Self-blame, guilt, cynicism and a sense of total failure set in.

- Anger and resentment at nothing in particular

- A feeling that something is missing

- You may find an extreme reluctance to go to work builds up, making it harder to face going to work each day, and particularly after a weekend or holiday.

- Self-confidence is lower

- Self-esteem is lower

- Sex drive is lower, or you can feel sexually unsatisfied

- Depression can set in

If stress is permitted to become established, it becomes a self-reinforcing process, giving rise to more and more negative actions and attitudes. This in turn leads to further stress and withdrawal. However, there is some good news. Learning how to handle stress will improve your quality of life. By keeping your stress under control, you will find that your health will improve. By improving your health, you will improve your ability to fight and control stress.

## Do not ignore the symptoms of stress

Worry related stress can affect people who, on the surface, appear relaxed and confident. One thing that you can be sure of is that you are not the only one suffering from stress. Chronic worries and acute worries are the two main types of worry. Most people experience a mixture of both chronic and acute worries at times of upset or stress. You may experience more of one type than the other.

Please read the following descriptions. See which one you recognise the most:

## Chronic worries

No matter how distracted you become, or how busy you are, your worries are never far from your thoughts. No matter how enjoyable things or activities used to be, chronic worries cast a dark cloud of gloom and despondency over everything that you do. Very severe chronic worries can lead to a general lack of interest in living, the loss of interest in the pleasures of life, a loss of the ability to enjoy things, and an inability to find pleasure in anything.

## Acute worries

Acute worries can come to mind unbidden and without any effort on your part. Something you've heard or seen can trigger off a chain of associations that are negative, at first below the level of consciousness.

Because this is going on below your level of consciousness, the stress may be overwhelming, even before you become aware of acute worries, leading to the condition referred to as *Awfulising*. This is where, by carrying the worry to absurd extremes, minor difficulties soon appear to be major problems. Hence the old term "Making a mountain out of a molehill".

The time that we are at our most vulnerable to attacks of both chronic and acute worrying is in the hours before dawn. (Do you find yourself waking at 3 or 4 am for no apparent reason?) Around this time of the morning our blood glucose levels, and temperature is low. The metabolism is sluggish, and our physical resistance is at its ebb. Our bodily state can and does exert a considerable influence over our moods. It is not surprising that any worries about relationships, career, money, health etc., chase each other endlessly around and around inside your head, thus driving sleep further and further away. You are now on the worry-go-round. This stress chapter may teach you how to get off that worry-go-round. Worry solves nothing. Learning to control your thoughts with meditation practice is also very highly recommended, see the meditation chapters.

## Monitoring your stress levels

It is important to monitor your stress levels. Most of us do not always appreciate how and why our stress levels have become so out of balance. Stress levels can rise rapidly, without you noticing that it is happening, until your physical and mental health has deteriorated to such a point that recovery is far harder. At times of over-stress, it can be extremely hard to put your finger on the precise nature of the problem; everything, work, life, just living, can become harder and harder to cope with, until you feel that there is not much that you can do about it.

On the other hand, you may be fully aware of the reasons why you are feeling so stressed, or apathetic, yet the feeling of being trapped by the causes of your difficulties can be so strong that you can become more stressed, making it appear difficult to do much about it. But there is something that we can all do about it, and that is to learn to control the negative effects of stress on our mind and body.

It is extremely important to monitor yourself for any build-up of the negative effects that stress can have upon you. By monitoring your stress levels, you can learn to avoid the build-up of unnecessary levels of stress. At times of crisis, or even a perceived crisis, you may get a sudden surge of the hormones Adrenaline, Noradrenaline and Cortisol into your bloodstream, giving rise to feelings of panic, fear, anxiety, and so on. At such times it can feel as if there is little or nothing you can do about it. On such occasions there is much that you can do to enable your mind and body to return as quickly as possible to normal running. Just by using the information in this stress management chapter you can soon learn to control your stress levels. When your body is suffering

from excess stress it sends out distress signals.
Listen to it. Do not ignore the signs that may be given
to you. Be Vigilant. It is essential to recognise the
symptoms of stress, and to take prompt action.

As well as the negative effects of stress listed in the
previous section, be aware of other warning signs,
such as:

- Breathing becomes shallow

- Heart rate goes up, and sometimes races

- Blood pressure goes up

- Blood sugar levels are increased

- You can at times feel detached from the world,
  on a high this is caused by too much
  Noradrenaline

- Being unable to perform work or tasks as well
  as you used to

- Your concentration becomes impaired,
  judgement is clouded

- You can become very irritable, agitated, for no
  apparent reason. This is caused by too much
  Adrenaline.

- You can gain an increasingly cynical outlook on
  life

- You may start to have a greater dependency

on alcohol, caffeine, nicotine or drugs.

- Your appetite can alter to either a desire to go on a binge, especially on sweet, sugary foods, or you may suffer a loss of all appetite

- Short-tempered

- Unusual clumsiness

- Chest pains.

- With extreme stress, bowels may loosen

- Feel depressed, tearful, irritable

- All over tension

- Excessive perspiration

How many of these signs do you recognise in yourself? Make a note of all of the warning signs that you recognise in your journal. And over the next three weeks or so watch as those feelings start to alter for the better.

By being able to deal with and control your stress, you will be able to do away with those excessive effects that are not good for you. Practice the calm technique and do not ignore the symptoms of stress.

Often people can appear to deal with some of the most dramatic crises in life: death of a loved one, redundancy, divorce etc, with very little sign of stress build up. This is often because one part of their life, at least, is continuing in a stable, positive way. We need balance in our lives, between work and play, but also in the other areas of life too. When you obtain a balance in those different areas, you will find that you can move through life in a calmer and less stressed way. Treating different areas of life with equal or near equal emphasis will help to balance those areas that include stressful situations.

**You can learn to control unnecessary worries.**

**Worry solves nothing.** The more you stand back and look at your worries from afar, the smaller they will become. A study carried out at Columbia University has produced scientific evidence to show that:

**Forty percent** of the things that you worry about never even happen, this is the what if this happens? What if that happens? scenario. We go looking for problems before they exist.

**Thirty percent** of your problems are over and done with before you even get around to worrying about them.

**Twelve percent** of our worries are about health problems that will never exist.

**Ten percent** of our worries are directed onto the wrong things.

As you can see, only 8% of your worries have any

substance to them. Because these worries are real, they need attention. Take control. Say to yourself, **"I am in control"**

You must give yourself time to worry. Actually, allocate some time, 20 to 30 minutes, and use this time to set strategies, define goals, make decisions. You will be able to look at your problems in a logical and analytical way. Be more constructive. Always stay within the allocated time. Once your worry time is over, tell your mind that it is now time to get on with life, (or sleep, if you are in bed). You are in control.

Whilst there is no single method that will work on its own to control the stress of worry, you can help yourself by using the information in this chapter to help you to control unnecessary worries, to learn self-relaxation, and to put your worries into perspective. And don't forget, regular meditation practice as I have written about in earlier chapters can hugely reduce stress.

**Here are some suggestions to help you manage unnecessary stress / worry:**

Learn the Calm Technique, as a positive tool for relaxation and change.

Stress has a part to play in your life - but so does "play". Take time for yourself to do other things outside of work, and outside of any situation in your life, which may be a cause of stress or worry.

Smoking. If you smoke, stop now. People who smoke think that at times of stress having a cigarette will calm them down. It won't. When you are suffering from stress the last thing you need is an adrenaline rush. Nicotine found in cigarettes is a powerful stimulant. Smoking starves your lungs, heart and brain of oxygen. It's no wonder so many smokers die from heart attacks so stop now!

## Exercise

One of the best ways to manage stress is to exercise. Exercise helps you to use up and burn off any of the stress hormones that may have built up to excess in your body. Even a little exercise is better than none at all, so get up off your couch and stop being a couch potato! By exercising you will become fitter. People who are physically fit can handle stress better.

Exercise helps to:

- Improve your lung capacity.

- Improve the blood flow to your brain.

- The extra oxygen and sugar in your blood helps with alertness and concentration.

- Flush out waste products more efficiently from your brain, and body.

- Increase endorphin production in your brain, making you feel good. It also increases electrical patterns (alpha waves) that may help with calmness.

- Lower fat (cholesterol) in your blood.

- Lower your blood pressure.

- Improve your heart efficiency.

- Increase blood flow around your body.

- Improve muscular function.

- Burn off the stress hormones Adrenaline, Noradrenaline and Cortisol, which will help you to stay calm.

If possible, visit a gym, or walk or run more, but before you undertake any exercise program that is new to you always seek professional advice from a qualified fitness instructor or talk to your own doctor.

**Make time**
Make time for loved ones. At times of excessive stress, we can forget that other people around us may be suffering as much as ourselves. If you have a friend or partner talk to them, but also listen to them. Keeping your fears and worries to yourself can often make them appear to be much worse than they are.

Make time for a social life; learn to balance those areas such as work and play. Make time for hobbies etc, but, above all, make time for **YOU.**

If you feel your body or mind slowing down, this is the time to take a short break from work or studies. Ideally, you should take a short break from work every

90 minutes, stopping all work activity, having a drink, but, if possible, leaving the place of work/study. Go for a walk - Just do something other than work. The idea is to give the brain a complete change of focus. This gives your mind a short rest.

After about 10 minutes, return to whatever you were doing, and you will see things afresh and be able to deal with things more efficiently. This is because your body and mind are back into a climb, on the curve towards peak performance.

Your mind needs time to focus on something completely different from work/study, even if only for a short time, so that, when returning, it is with a renewed strength and alertness.

Do not take your meals, or breaks, at your desk or workbench. Mealtimes and breaks are an ideal time to unwind, that is why we have them. If you stay at your place of work for meals, your mind does not get a break. At a subconscious level the mind is still looking at what remains to be done, it is still worrying, plus, you are still next to your phone and computer

**Diet and Stress**
There are some foods and drinks that can aggravate stress levels or even kick start your stress reaction. Research has shown that people who don't have breakfast are more likely to be far more tired at the end of the day. So always start your day with something to eat. Have three meals a day. When you are under stress your immune system is often not

working as well as it should. Eating plenty of fresh fruit and vegetables gives you the vitamin C to help your immune system function more efficiently. Eat a balanced diet. Eat complex carbohydrates, such as pasta, jacket potatoes, and wholemeal bread. Do not eat refined, pre-prepared foods, which often have a lot of salt and/or sugar in them. This can help to stop stress mood swings.

At times of stress you can sweat excessively. This in turn can lead to dehydration. You need to drink plenty of water to help with rehydration. Drinking alcohol to excess can heighten stress levels, so only drink alcohol in moderation. Caffeine is a stimulant, so keep your consumption of drinks like coffee, tea, chocolate, and soft drinks like cola, down to a minimum. Drink water. Be aware that stopping your caffeine intake abruptly can cause severe headaches. Cut back on the amount you drink slowly over several days.

If you are unsure of your diet, always consult a dietician or your own doctor.

In three to four weeks, most people start to feel the difference in their energy levels. They have more energy, less muscle aches and better sleep.

At lunch time, have a light meal - drink little if any alcohol, even if it is a business lunch. This helps to avoid the post lunch lethargy.

When having meals at home, have them at the table and not on a tray in front of the television or similar device. Leave your mobile phone on silent somewhere away from the table. You will find that this helps you to unwind, and gives you the opportunity, if you have a partner / family, to talk to them without the interference of the television or your mobile phone. Mealtimes are an ideal time for families to be together. It can be a time for social activity. A time to talk, to communicate with others. Use this time, not just to eat, but also to interact with others. You may be pleasantly surprised at how your perception of your problems and the world around you can change for the better, just by communicating with others.

Remember, stress has a part to play in your life, but so does play. So make time for yourself. Have some fun!

**Control your Breathing. Control your Stress**
We can survive for three weeks without food. We can survive for 3 days without water. Without air we are dead within 3 minutes, Dr. Sheldon S. Hendle maintains that we have 75 trillion cells in our bodies, and that each one of these cells is breathing. The words 75 trillion may have little meaning to most people (that is 75,000,000,000,000,000,000,000), but you will appreciate that is a lot of cells to keep topped up with air!

We breathe at a normal rate of between 12 and 16 breaths a minute. Men breathe slightly slower than women at between 12 to 14 breaths a minute. Women breathe at 14 to16 breaths a minute. At times of stress the way that you breathe changes, your rate of breathing may increase to such a rapid level that you may start to hyperventilate. You may even find that your breathing momentarily ceases. This happens to give your body the chance to recover and to return to a more normal rate of breathing.

At such times of altered breathing, you will start to use only the upper portions of your lungs, resulting in your breathing becoming very rapid and shallow. This type of breathing is called hyperventilation. Panic attacks are always accompanied by hyperventilation.

The bottom of the lungs has the most blood flow, approximately one litre per minute. The top has approximately 0.1 of a litres per minute, ten times less than the bottom of the lungs. So, it is important to get as much air down to the bottom of the lungs as we can. However, we must do it in a slow, controlled way, because during rapid, shallow breathing most of the air only reaches the upper and middle parts of the lungs. Because of this altered state of breathing, the body attempts to draw even more air into the lungs. This results in much more oxygen than the body can cope with getting into the bloodstream.

Because of breathing out very fast, far more carbon dioxide than usual is washed out of the bloodstream, resulting in the blood becoming slightly more alkaline. We end up with a pH. imbalance. An imbalance in the ratio of oxygen to carbon dioxide in the blood takes place, i.e., more oxygen and less carbon dioxide.

Momentarily holding your breath in response to stress will also lead quickly to a build-up of carbon dioxide. This produces physical and mental symptoms as equally distressing as those caused by hyperventilation.

The anxiety and symptoms produced by these sorts of breathing triggers a vicious cycle in which our stress levels go up. Sudden changes in our breathing patterns can cause distressing effects such as dizziness, fast heartbeat and pains in the chest. These chest pains are caused by the muscles between the ribs going into painful spasm, which can make some people think that they are on the verge of a heart attack. Feelings of panic can overcome you, anxiety levels rise, your physical and intellectual performance can be diminished, nightmares are increased, your sleep can become disturbed, you can suffer from disturbed vision, and at times may even have hallucinations. You can have sensations of unreality; the palms of your hands can sweat more than "normal". Underarm sweating can also increase.

Because of this altered state of breathing, your body has to work much harder to maintain the required level of gas exchange in the lungs. Also, remember that you have 75 trillion cells to keep going.

At such times, there can be so much oxygen in the blood that the person suffering the panic attack can faint. This gives the body the chance to stop breathing, for up to a minute, and thus give time for the gas levels in the blood to return to normal. Whilst this can be very frightening for anyone who witnesses such an attack, the condition will start to reverse itself as soon as the sufferer regains consciousness. Young people are more susceptible to fainting.

Shallow breathing is a primitive mechanism for survival, to give us the ability for fight or flight, but today we very rarely must stand and fight, nor do we have the opportunity to run away from any stressful situations that we find ourselves in. In fact, we do not always know what it is that we want to run away from. So, we freeze. Because of this, we do not use up the powerful chemicals Adrenaline and Noradrenalin that are released into our bloodstream, and our physical tension rises sharply.

By contrast, slow, deep breathing, using your diaphragm, uses all of your lungs. By using all of your lung capacity you get the air to the lower parts of the lungs, which are richest in blood vessels, enabling the process of expansion and ventilation to occur more efficiently.

This deep breathing helps to maintain the correct balance between the gases in the blood, whilst giving you additional oxygen. It also helps to stimulate your body to produce mood-boosting Endorphins.

Endorphins are morphine-like substances produced naturally in the body. They have a wide range of functions. They help to regulate the action of the heart. They help with the perception of pain. It is probable that they are involved in controlling emotions, mood and motivation. It is thought that they are produced at times that the body needs help in the relief of acute pain or mental distress.

Deep, slow breathing aids relaxation, reduces tension, and gives you a much greater sense of control over yourself, and a greater feeling of physical and mental wellbeing.

So, breathe deeply, breathe slowly!

---

**Therapy Journal exercise 2**

Now write in your journal how you plan to deal with and reduce your stress levels

Keep a record of your progress.

Take the stress test again in 4 weeks' time to check your progress.

Now go to the Introduction to Meditation chapter

**Initial Consultation > Journal > Fast Help > Stress Management > Introduction to Meditation >**

---

# 11. Personal Development

*"If you plan on being anything less than you are capable of being. You will probably be unhappy all the days of your life".* Abraham Maslow

## Personal Development

Imagine a ship setting out to sea with no plan of where it was going, it would soon run aground. Imagine building a house with no building plans! So, if we want to achieve anything in life, we need to set ourselves goals and plan how we are going to achieve them. You need to visualise your goals every morning as though you already had achieved them. It is recommended that you write down your goals and read them first thing in the morning and last thing at night.

First thing when you get up in the morning. Think how you can make the day interesting and exciting. See the day's events having a positive outcome. Re-write your major goals. Spend the first 20mins in the morning to program your mind with inspirational information.

Last thing at night just before you fall asleep visualise your goal's as if you had attained them. See yourself as the person you really want to be. Visualise the next day going the way you want it. Mentally rehearse the outcome of important events.

Act continuously as though you already had the qualities you desire. Form a clear mental picture of yourself as you want to be. There are 3 ways to help with this.

## 1. Affirmations:

Positive present tense affirmations with feeling and enthusiasm. They must be personal, positive and in the present tense.

Here are 3 good affirmations:

Look in the mirror and say to yourself "I like myself" and visualise all the good things about yourself. This is a good way of overcoming a poor self-image inherited during childhood. Use this affirmation as often as possible.

When you wake up in the morning say to yourself "I feel fantastic" and visualise yourself feeling fantastic. This will set you up for the day. Most people get up and immediately look forward to going back to bed!

When faced with a negative emotion say to yourself "I am responsible". This has an immediate effect of cancelling out the negative emotion.

## 2. Visualization

Form a clear picture of what you want continuously. Visualise it as if it has already happened. Act the part of the person you would like to be. If you are not happy in a situation, PRETEND the situation is exciting, then it will change to being so. If you are in a boring situation PRETEND it is interesting. Think how to make a situation interesting.

You need to practice positive thoughts continuously to form a new habit; in the absence of positive thoughts weeds will grow!

### 3. Be prepared to let go of the past
Remember:

If you think you are beaten, you are.

If you think you dare not, you do not.

If you would like to win, but you think you cannot, it is almost certain you will not.

*Thinking makes it so!*

# Making your Dreams a Reality

There are no such things as unrealistic goals, only unrealistic time frames. Some experts believe fully that 80 percent of all problems in personal and business life come from a lack of clarity with regard to our objectives and goals. The word "goals" can be intimidating, it can feel so overbearing that it keeps people from beginning the process. Therefore, it is helpful to pretend you are a child again when you are thinking about your goals. What child do you know who does not have a million things he or she wants to do?

Many people will tell you to write down your goals but not have 100 as your target number of goals. However, you cannot have too many goals. Here is why:

Goals have different gestation periods. Some are

accomplished quickly; some take many years.

When we reach a goal, it loses power and importance for us. We need plenty more to keep our conscious and subconscious mind at work!

The rule of the universe is abundance. Since you can have almost everything you really want, why settle for less?

Do your goals have to be accomplished tomorrow? Next week? This year? Of course not! Your goals can be added to, subtracted from, and achieved as you move through life.

## Create your Own Dream List

Let your mind float freely. Imagine that you have no limitations. Imagine that you have all the time, money, all the resources, intelligence, all the education, all the experience and all the contacts in the world. Imagine that you could do, be or have anything in your life.

Write down everything you would want in your life if you had no limitations whatsoever on your potential, as if you have had no fear of failure at all.

It is helpful to imagine that whatever you write down you are guaranteed to receive. Be sure to decide what you want before you limit yourself in advance by thinking of all the reasons why it is not possible. Put the word possible aside for now and just allow yourself to dream.

You might also imagine that you had just been given £10 million (tax-free). How would you change your life? What would you buy?

It might help if you also consider the following two questions:

1. What makes you unhappy? Ask yourself "In what situations in my life, and with whom, am I not perfectly happy?" Force yourself to think about every part of your day, from morning to night, and write down every element that makes you unhappy or dissatisfied in any way. Remember, proper diagnosis is half the cure. Identifying the unsatisfactory situations is the first step to resolving them.

2. What makes you happy? In looking over your life, where and when have you been the happiest? Where were you, and what were you doing?

# Goal Guidelines

Here is a checklist to ensure you are using a successful framework to set your goals:

Your most important goals must be yours. Not your partners. Not your child's. Not your employer's. Yours. When you let other people determine your definition of success, you are sabotaging your own future.

Your goals must mean something to you. Your reasons for charting a new course of action give you the drive and energy to get up every morning.

Your goals must be specific and measurable. Vague generalisations and wishy-washy statements are not good enough. Be extremely specific! The more details and precise adjectives and timing you insert the more likely it will occur.

Write down your goals in positive terms. Avoid saying I will *not* be. Your subconscious is extremely specific, and it filters out the negative and will attract like a powerful magnet all the negative things you write down.

Your goals must be in the present tense. Avoid saying I *will* have. Write down your goals as if you had your dream today and right now. This will help keep time from sabotaging your achievements.

Your goals must be flexible. A flexible plan keeps you from feeling suffocated and allows you to take advantage of genuine opportunities that walk in your future door.

Your goals must be challenging and exciting. Force yourself to jump out of your comfort zone to acquire that much-needed energy and edge.

Your goals must be in alignment with your values. Pay attention to your intuition and your gut feelings. When you set a goal that contradicts your values, you will feel uncomfortable.

Your goals must be well balanced. Make sure you include areas that allow time to relax, have fun and enjoy.

Your goals must be realistic and achievable.

**Initial Consultation > Journal > Fast Help > Stress Management > Introduction to Meditation > Altered State Meditation > Personal Development > Memory Recall Therapy >**

# 12. The Spiritual Part

*"All I want to do is think like God"*
The scientist, Albert Einstein

In the meditation section of this book I wrote about practicing self separation. So, your higher self is observing the false part, the negative emotions, or feelings. In meditation self separation also involves your higher self silently observing other things such as your thoughts, parts of your body and virtually anything else its attention is directed too. You will see that there must be at least two parts of you if one part is observing the other.

One of the aims of meditation is detachment from the notion that your thoughts are you and that is all there is to you. There is much more to you. Consciousness calibration research has shown that ninety-nine percent of the mind is silent. Your thoughts are associated to and influenced by your personality and ego. And so, could be grouped together as your conscious mind and subconscious mind. Leaving the other part of you, your higher self.  The great masters going back over three thousand years and beyond, to the Vedic ancient knowledge say that meditation is designed to contact the higher self, the spiritual self, or soul.

So now we have the higher self grouped with the spiritual self, or soul. It is in fact the one and the same. This is the real you I have written about earlier. I am just adding information here about it now we have reached this spiritual chapter! It is the part of you that never dies, the eternal part of you. To give you an analogy, the ego and personality of a person are like the transient waves on top of an ocean whilst the higher self, spiritual self or soul is like the deep still ocean underneath. However, most people's perception is firmly seated in the waves. So, the person thinks that they are the waves! To put it another way, most people think that they are their personality, when in fact they are comprised of so much more! The personality is not eternal, but the higher self is!

What I have written above, is well known ancient spiritual knowledge which you can check out by reading the books listed in the bibliography section of this book. Later, you will see how quantum science and physics supports much of what the spiritual masters have been saying. However, depending on your beliefs, current life history and where you are in the scheme of things, you may find it hard to accept what I have written above. That being the case, which of the two possibilities below makes you feel good?

- You are an eternal higher self/spiritual self/soul and so are currently an infinite consciousness having an experience as (*insert your name here*).
- It is just you, flesh and bones and personality, that is all there is. When your dead that is it, you are gone for ever!

I would suggest the first one! So why not at least take it on board as a theory for now, as it will make you feel so much better!

Moving on, this higher self of yours has a connection to an intelligent creative cosmic force which different cultures throughout history have given different names. These include God, but the definition of "God" has often been slightly distorted by some religions to maintain control over their worshipers.

Carl Jung said "*One of the main functions of organised religion is to protect people against a direct experience of God*". So, lets define God as an infinite non personal, non-judgmental and the highest spiritual creative force located on a plane of existence beyond the physical plane. In fact, the physical plane is created from this higher cosmic plane. Before the advent of modern quantum science, it used to be just the spiritual masters claiming this. Now this is confirmed by quantum science / quantum mechanics.

Here is a brief simplified explanation. As we look at matter, we find molecules then atoms, then electrons, then subatomic particles and then sub-subatomic particles. Ultimately, if we were to place these tiny quantum subatomic particles into a particle accelerator and collide them trying to find their source. We would discover what famous scientists such as Albert Einstein and Max Planck discovered.

## Max Planck

Max Planck received the noble prize in Stockholm Sweden in 1918 for his work on the atom. He was considered to be the greatest scientific mind of his time. Much later in a speech in Florence, Italy in 1944 he made the following speech:

*"As a man who has devoted his whole life to the most clear headed science, to the study of matter, I can tell you as a result of my research about atoms this much: There is no matter as such. All matter originates and exists only by virtue of a force which brings the particles of an atom to vibration and holds this most minute solar system of the atom together. We must assume behind this force the existence of a conscious and intelligent spirit. This spirit is the matrix of all matter, it is the source of all matter and you listening, you here in this room, all of us are made up of particles that we call matter"*

Another quote by Max Planck; *"In all my research I have never come across matter. To me the term matter implies a bundle of energy which is given form by an intelligent spirit".*

## Albert Einstein

Albert Einstein had come to the same conclusion

when he said *"All I want to do is think like God"*

Three further quotes by Albert Einstein: *"We are slowed down sound and light waves, a walking bundle of frequencies tuned into the cosmos. We are souls dressed up in sacred biochemical garments and our bodies are the instruments through which our souls play their music".*

*"The more I study science, the more I believe in God".*

*"I want to know all Gods thoughts; all the rest are just details".*

## David Bohm

The theoretical physicist David Bohm is mostly known for his work in quantum physics. But he also deeply explored the nature of thought and consciousness. Here are four of his quotes relevant to what I am trying to explain here:

*"Ultimately, the entire universe has to be understood as a single undivided whole".*

*"Thought creates our world, and then says, 'I didn't do it".*

*"To change your reality, you have to change your inner thoughts".*

*"We are internally related to everything, not [just] externally related. Consciousness is an internal relationship to the whole, we take in the whole, and we act toward the whole. Whatever we have taken in determines basically what we are. Wholeness is a*

*kind of attitude or approach to the whole of life. If we can have a coherent approach to reality, then reality will respond coherently to us".*

In quantum science, the observer influences the experiment, this has been demonstrated in a number of experiments including the double slit experiment.

Therefore, we have eminent quantum scientists and spiritual gurus coming to a consensus that there is a higher (non-personal) spiritual cosmic intelligence often called God behind all creation (including us) and that we are part of that creation and therefore, can influence creation with our own thoughts. Your higher self, the real you, the part that is timeless and eternal is part of this force often called God. And being the higher and real and eternal part of you, has a much stronger connection to "God". When you enter a thoughtless state in meditation this is called transcendence. You then gain direct connection to your higher self and the higher spiritual force often called "God". You do not need to be an experienced meditator for this to happen, you only need to be in this thoughtless state for seconds to transcend and reap the benefits.

Through continued use of the right type of meditation such as Vedic Meditation as explained in this book, the higher self seems to become more integrated with one's personality. Benefits of this include a much more relaxed outlook on life where the things that used to stress you no longer bother you. You also begin to develop an understanding that we are all ultimately connected to each other. This greatly improves our interactions with other people. There is an old native American proverb that says *"No tree has branches so foolish as to fight amongst themselves"*

Why am I telling you all this? What did Albert Einstein mean when he said *"All I want to do is think like God"*? If you understand the laws or the operating system of God / cosmic creative force, work with them and incorporate them into your life, you are going to have an easy time. Just like sitting in a boat flowing with the direction of the river. Working against the way the cosmic creative force works, will mean life will be like trying to paddle up the oncoming water of the river. Best to go with the flow and force!

An example would be to get creative in a hobby or occupation that really interests you. This cosmic creative force is always creating and therefore you are in the flow. If being creative involves something which you are good at and really inspires you, you are inspired ... in spirit. As I wrote in an earlier chapter, this helps greatly with anxiety and mental health problems. Spending time in nature which I also wrote about earlier, helps with mental health problems, as you are closer to God, the creative cosmic force.

If you wish to be in harmony with the power of God, the creative cosmic force and go with the flow for an easier life, in addition to being creative, be kind to yourself and others. A fundamental attribute of the creative cosmic force is kindness. All that is manifested is brought here to thrive, this takes a kindly power. Also, do not judge others, this creative force does not judge. So, if you find yourself judging others you are going against the natural creative flow of life.

So, coming back to meditation. Our aim is to still the mind, to obtain some silence and space between our thoughts. Creation and matter come from space and silence. If you look out of your window and see a tree, it came from a seed, made up of particles such as electrons and subatomic quarks. These came from the void/space/silence as documented by the aforementioned quantum scientists, as the result of a spiritual intelligent force often called God. Saint Paul said "… that which is seen hath not come from what doth appear,". What he meant was, matter does not produce matter, it comes from the emptiness, void, and silence I have written about in this chapter. The silence between our thoughts. That is why entering the transcendence state of no thoughts in meditation even if only for a few seconds, is so beneficial on many levels.

Finally, now at the end of this book, I will leave you with two considerations and would suggest that you remember them always, wherever you are and whatever you find yourself experiencing:

You are a powerful infinite eternal consciousness currently having an experience as …. (insert your name here).

*"We tend to forget that happiness doesn't come as a result of getting something we don't have, but rather recognising and appreciating what we do have"*

Frederick Koenig

---

**Initial Consultation > Journal > Fast Help > Stress Management > Introduction to Meditation > Altered State Meditation >  Thought & Emotion Control Meditation  > Spiritual Part > Personal Development > Memory & Emotion Recall**

---

Make sure you go to the first page of the Appendix to get support information and to find out how to download the free relaxation audio.

If you have found this book helpful, or even if you didn't, I would love to hear your comments about it. You can leave your thoughts on the website where you purchased this book.

# Appendix Section

## APPENDIX 1

## Free Downloads & Support

To listen to the free relaxation audio program for use with the stress management chapter, visit my authors website at **www.healthyandwise.co.uk** and go to the Therapy for your Mind book page.

At the time of writing on the 29th December 2020, I plan to make a free newsletter available to keep you updated with the availability of additional resources, such as additional support by the way of further audio downloads, therapist support and a low-cost member therapy support program. This will be under the umbrella of the Mind Therapy Society. Details will be on my website **www.healthyandwise.co.uk** and/or searching for the Mind Therapy Society. You can contact me by email at paul@healthyandwise.co.uk

## APPENDIX 2

# Visual Mindful Meditation Practice

The following visualisation mindfulness meditation can be practiced daily at any time for 15 minutes when you are sitting alone, comfortable and will not be disturbed. However, as you are likely already practicing the easy Altered State / Vedic meditation, you could practice this one to help you get to sleep if your mind is still very alert. I would not recommend this as a standalone meditation as the Vedic one is much easier. However, this visualisation mindfulness meditation compliments the Vedic meditation and will speed up your therapy.  It is in two parts as below:

### Part 1: Relaxation module

1. Sit upright on your chair with your head erect with your feet a few inches apart. Your hands on your thighs, held loosely together on your lap or resting gently by your side.
2. If you are using this to relax your mind before sleep in bed, relax and lie down on your bed in preparation for sleep and turn out the light.
3. Look upward slightly and fix your eyes on a spot either real or imaginary in front of you.

4. Tell yourself you are going to silently count to 3 and on the count of 3, your eyes will close, and you will begin to relax.

5. Now count to 3 and let your eyes close.

6. Start your relaxation by fixing your attention on your feet. Begin with your toes, curl your toes, and let them go, notice the sensation as they relax. Let the relaxation rise up into both of your feet. Notice the sensation in your feet.

7. Tense and relax your legs below your knees. Then allow the relaxation to flow up into your calf muscles. Take your time to sense the feeling in your calf muscles.

8. Let the relaxation rise up over your thighs and let both of your legs relax.

9. Now fix your attention on your stomach, relax every muscle, every nerve and every fibre in your stomach as your stomach rests.

10. Now focus on your chest, notice how each deep breath is relaxing you more and more.

11. Now place your attention on your hands and your arms. Begin with your fingers, tightly close your fingers, pause, then open them and feel your hands, relax. Let that relaxation rise up through your hands, wrists, forearms and upper arms. Take your time, notice the physical sensations as your hands, wrists, forearms and upper arms progressively relax.

12. Let that relaxation sweep across your shoulders, notice any areas of tension or tightness in your shoulders, and let it go.

13. Let the relaxation rise up the back of your head, across the top of your head and down to

your forehead. Relax your forehead and let any real or imaginary wrinkles go. Now down to your eyes, cheeks, mouth and chin. Let your jaw and whole face relax.

## Part 2: Special place module

Select a special place where you would like to explore. It could be a place you have been on holiday, a place in the country, one of your favourite walks, a garden, a special room or building. Ideally it should be a place you have been to and love and can spend time visualising and exploring it in your mind. You could also make up an imaginary special place and spend time exploring that imaginary place. Get creative!

# Appendix 3

## List of Phobias

Ablutophobia- Fear of washing or bathing.

Acarophobia- Fear of itching or of the insects that cause itching.

Acerophobia- Fear of sourness.

Achluophobia- Fear of darkness.

Acousticophobia- Fear of noise.

Acrophobia- Fear of heights.

Aerophobia- Fear of drafts, air swallowing, or airborne noxious substances.

Aeroacrophobia- Fear of open high places.

Aeronausiphobia- Fear of vomiting secondary to airsickness.

Agateophobia- Fear of insanity.

Agliophobia- Fear of pain.

Agoraphobia- Fear of open spaces or of being in crowded, public places like markets. Fear of leaving a safe place.

Agrizoophobia- Fear of wild animals.

Agyrophobia- Fear of streets or crossing the street.

Aichmophobia- Fear of needles or pointed objects.

Ailurophobia- Fear of cats.

Albuminurophobia- Fear of kidney disease.

Alektorophobia- Fear of chickens.

Algophobia- Fear of pain.

Alliumphobia- Fear of garlic.

Allodoxaphobia- Fear of opinions.

Altophobia- Fear of heights.

Amathophobia- Fear of dust.

Amaxophobia- Fear of riding in a car.

Ambulophobia- Fear of walking.

Amnesiphobia- Fear of amnesia.

Amychophobia- Fear of scratches or being scratched.

Anablephobia- Fear of looking up.

Ancraophobia- Fear of wind. (Anemophobia)

Androphobia- Fear of men.

Anemophobia- Fear of air drafts or wind.
(Ancraophobia)

Anginophobia- Fear of angina, choking or
narrowness.

Angrophobia – Fear of anger or of becoming angry.

Anthrophobia or Anthophobia- Fear of flowers.

Anthropophobia- Fear of people or society.

Antlophobia- Fear of floods.

Anuptaphobia- Fear of staying single.

Apeirophobia- Fear of infinity.

Aphenphosmphobia- Fear of being touched.
(Haphephobia)

Apiphobia- Fear of bees.

Apotemnophobia- Fear of persons with amputations.

Arachnephobia or Arachnophobia- Fear of spiders.

Arithmophobia- Fear of numbers.

Arrhenphobia- Fear of men.

Arsonphobia- Fear of fire.

Asthenophobia- Fear of fainting or weakness.

Astraphobia or Astrapophobia- Fear of thunder and
lightning.(Ceraunophobia, Keraunophobia)

Astrophobia- Fear of stars or celestial space.

Asymmetriphobia- Fear of asymmetrical things.
Ataxiophobia- Fear of ataxia. (muscular incoordination)
Ataxophobia- Fear of disorder or untidiness.
Atelophobia- Fear of imperfection.
Atephobia- Fear of a ruin or ruins.
Athazagoraphobia- Fear of being forgotten or ignored or forgetting.
Atomosophobia- Fear of atomic explosions.
Autodysomophobia- Fear of one that has a vile odour.
Automatonophobia- Fear of ventriloquist's dummies, animatronic creatures, wax statues – anything that falsely represents a sentient being.
Automysophobia- Fear of being dirty.
Autophobia- Fear of being alone or of oneself.
Aviophobia or Aviatophobia- Fear of flying.

Bacillophobia- Fear of microbes.
Bacteriophobia- Fear of bacteria.
Basophobia or Basiphobia- Inability to stand. Fear of walking or falling.
Bathmophobia- Fear of stairs or steep slopes.
Bathophobia- Fear of depth.
Batophobia- Fear of heights or being close to high buildings.
Batrachophobia- Fear of amphibians, such as frogs, newts, salamanders, etc.
Belonephobia- Fear of pins and needles. (Aichmophobia)
Bibliophobia- Fear of books.
Blennophobia- Fear of slime.

Botanophobia- Fear of plants.

Bromidrosiphobia or Bromidrophobia- Fear of body smells.

Brontophobia- Fear of thunder and lightning.

Bufonophobia- Fear of toads.

Cacophobia- Fear of ugliness.

Cainophobia or Cainotophobia- Fear of newness, novelty.

Caligynephobia- Fear of beautiful women.

Cancerophobia or Carcinophobia- Fear of cancer.

Cardiophobia- Fear of the heart.

Carnophobia- Fear of meat.

Catagelophobia- Fear of being ridiculed.

Catapedaphobia- Fear of jumping from high and low places.

Cathisophobia- Fear of sitting.

Catoptrophobia- Fear of mirrors.

Cenophobia or Centophobia- Fear of new things or ideas.

Ceraunophobia or Keraunophobia- Fear of thunder and lightning.(Astraphobia, Astrapophobia)

Chaetophobia- Fear of hair.

Cheimaphobia or Cheimatophobia- Fear of cold.(Frigophobia, Psychophobia)

Chemophobia- Fear of chemicals or working with chemicals.

Chionophobia- Fear of snow.

Chorophobia- Fear of dancing.

Chrometophobia or Chrematophobia- Fear of money.

Chromophobia or Chromatophobia- Fear of colours.

Chronophobia- Fear of time.

Chronomentrophobia- Fear of clocks.

Cibophobia- Fear of food.(Sitophobia, Sitiophobia)

Claustrophobia- Fear of confined spaces.

Cleithrophobia or Cleisiophobia- Fear of being locked in an enclosed place.

Cleptophobia- Fear of stealing.

Climacophobia- Fear of stairs, climbing, or of falling downstairs.

Clinophobia- Fear of going to bed.

Clithrophobia or Cleithrophobia- Fear of being enclosed.

Cnidophobia- Fear of stings.

Coimetrophobia- Fear of cemeteries.

Coprastasophobia- Fear of constipation.

Consecotaleophobia- Fear of chopsticks.

Coulrophobia- Fear of clowns.

Counterphobia- The preference by a phobic for fearful situations.

Cremnophobia- Fear of precipices.

Cryophobia- Fear of extreme cold, ice or frost.

Crystallophobia- Fear of crystals or glass.

Cyberphobia- Fear of computers or working on a computer.

Cyclophobia- Fear of bicycles.

Cymophobia or Kymophobia- Fear of waves or wave like motions.

Cynophobia- Fear of dogs or rabies.

Decidophobia- Fear of making decisions.

Defecaloesiophobia- Fear of painful bowels

movements.

Deipnophobia- Fear of dining or dinner conversations.

Dementophobia- Fear of insanity.

Demonophobia or Daemonophobia- Fear of demons.

Demophobia- Fear of crowds. (Agoraphobia)

Dendrophobia- Fear of trees.

Dentophobia- Fear of dentists.

Dermatophobia- Fear of skin lesions.

Dermatosiophobia or Dermatophobia or Dermatopathophobia- Fear of skin disease.

Dextrophobia- Fear of objects at the right side of the body.

Diabetophobia- Fear of diabetes.

Didaskaleinophobia- Fear of going to school.

Dikephobia- Fear of justice.

Dinophobia- Fear of dizziness or whirlpools.

Diplophobia- Fear of double vision.

Dipsophobia- Fear of drinking.

Dishabiliophobia- Fear of undressing in front of someone.

Domatophobia- Fear of houses or being in a house.(Eicophobia, Oikophobia)

Doraphobia- Fear of fur or skins of animals.

Doxophobia- Fear of expressing opinions or of receiving praise.

Dromophobia- Fear of crossing streets.

Dysmorphophobia- Fear of deformity.

Dystychiphobia- Fear of accidents.

Eicophobia- Fear of home surroundings. (Domatophobia, Oikophobia)

Eisoptrophobia- Fear of mirrors or of seeing oneself in a mirror.

Electrophobia- Fear of electricity.

Eleutherophobia- Fear of freedom.

Elurophobia- Fear of cats. (Ailurophobia)

Emetophobia- Fear of vomiting.

Enetophobia- Fear of pins.

Enochlophobia- Fear of crowds.

Enosiophobia or Enissophobia- Fear of having committed an unpardonable sin or of criticism.

Entomophobia- Fear of insects.

Eosophobia- Fear of dawn or daylight.

Ephebiphobia- Fear of teenagers.

Epistaxiophobia- Fear of nosebleeds.

Epistemophobia- Fear of knowledge.

Equinophobia- Fear of horses.

Eremophobia- Fear of being oneself or of loneliness.

Ereuthrophobia- Fear of blushing.

Ergasiophobia- 1) Fear of work or functioning. 2) Surgeon's fear of operating.

Ergophobia- Fear of work.

Erotophobia- Fear of sexual love or sexual questions.

Euphobia- Fear of hearing good news.

Erythrophobia or Erytophobia or Ereuthophobia- 1) Fear of redlights. 2) Blushing. 3) Red.

Febriphobia or Fibriphobia or Fibriophobia- Fear of fever.

Felinophobia- Fear of cats. (Ailurophobia, Elurophobia, Galeophobia, Gatophobia)

Francophobia- Fear of France or French culture. (Gallophobia, Galiophobia)

Frigophobia- Fear of cold or cold things. (Cheimaphobia, Cheimatophobia, Psychrophobia)

Galeophobia or Gatophobia- Fear of cats.

Geliophobia- Fear of laughter.

Gelotophobia- Fear of being laughed at.

Geniophobia- Fear of chins.

Genophobia- Fear of sex.

Genuphobia- Fear of knees.

Gephyrophobia or Gephydrophobia or Gephysrophobia- Fear of crossing bridges.

Gerascophobia- Fear of growing old.

Gerontophobia- Fear of old people or of growing old.

Geumaphobia or Geumophobia- Fear of taste.

Glossophobia- Fear of speaking in public or of trying to speak.

Gnosiophobia- Fear of knowledge.

Graphophobia- Fear of writing or handwriting.

Gymnophobia- Fear of nudity.

Gynephobia or Gynophobia- Fear of women.

Hadephobia- Fear of hell.

Hagiophobia- Fear of saints or holy things.

Hamartophobia- Fear of sinning.

Haphephobia or Haptephobia Fear of being touched.

Harpaxophobia- Fear of being robbed.

Hedonophobia- Fear of feeling pleasure.

Heliophobia- Fear of the sun.

Hemophobia or Hemaphobia or Hematophobia- Fear of blood.

Herpetophobia- Fear of reptiles or creepy, crawly things.

Heterophobia- Fear of the opposite sex. (Sexophobia)

Hexakosioihexekontahexaphobia- Fear of the number 666.

Hierophobia- Fear of priests or sacred things.

Hippophobia- Fear of horses.

Hodophobia- Fear of road travel.

Hormephobia- Fear of shock.

Homichlophobia- Fear of fog.

Homilophobia- Fear of sermons.

Hominophobia- Fear of men.

Homophobia- Fear of sameness, monotony or of homosexuality or of becoming homosexual.

Hoplophobia- Fear of firearms.

Hydrargyophobia- Fear of mercurial medicines.

Hydrophobia- Fear of water or of rabies.

Hydrophobophobia- Fear of rabies.

Hyelophobia or Hyalophobia- Fear of glass.

Hygrophobia- Fear of liquids, dampness, or moisture.

Hylephobia- Fear of materialism or the fear of epilepsy.

Hylophobia- Fear of forests.

Hypengyophobia or Hypegiaphobia- Fear of responsibility.

Hypnophobia- Fear of sleep or of being hypnotised.

Hypsiphobia- Fear of height.

Iatrophobia- Fear of going to the doctor or of doctors.

Ichthyophobia- Fear of fish.

Ideophobia- Fear of ideas.

Illyngophobia- Fear of vertigo or feeling dizzy when looking down.

Iophobia- Fear of poison.

Insectophobia – Fear of insects.

Isolophobia- Fear of solitude, being alone.

Isopterophobia- Fear of termites, insects that eat wood.

Japanophobia- Fear of Japanese.

Judeophobia- Fear of Jews.

Kainolophobia or Kainophobia- Fear of anything new, novelty.

Katagelophobia- Fear of ridicule.

Kathisophobia- Fear of sitting down.

Kenophobia- Fear of voids or empty spaces.

Keraunophobia or Ceraunophobia- Fear of thunder and lightning.(Astraphobia, Astrapophobia)

Kinetophobia or Kinesophobia- Fear of movement or motion.

Kolpophobia- Fear of genitals, particularly female.

Kopophobia- Fear of fatigue.

Koniophobia- Fear of dust. (Amathophobia)

Kosmikophobia- Fear of cosmic phenomenon.

Kymophobia- Fear of waves. (Cymophobia)

Kynophobia- Fear of rabies.

Kyphophobia- Fear of stooping.

Lachanophobia- Fear of vegetables.

Laliophobia or Lalophobia- Fear of speaking.

Leukophobia- Fear of the colour white.

Levophobia- Fear of things to the left side of the body.

Ligyrophobia- Fear of loud noises.

Lilapsophobia- Fear of tornadoes and hurricanes.

Limnophobia- Fear of lakes.

Linonophobia- Fear of string.

Liticaphobia- Fear of lawsuits.

Lockiophobia- Fear of childbirth.

Logizomechanophobia- Fear of computers.

Luiphobia- Fear of lues, syphillis.

Lutraphobia- Fear of otters.

Lygophobia- Fear of darkness.

Lyssophobia- Fear of rabies or of becoming mad.

Macrophobia- Fear of long waits.

Maieusiophobia- Fear of childbirth.

Malaxophobia- Fear of love play. (Sarmassophobia)

Maniaphobia- Fear of insanity.

Mastigophobia- Fear of punishment.

Mechanophobia- Fear of machines.

Megalophobia- Fear of large things.

Melissophobia- Fear of bees.

Melanophobia- Fear of the colour black.

Melophobia- Fear or hatred of music.

Meningitophobia- Fear of brain disease.

Menophobia- Fear of menstruation.

Merinthophobia- Fear of being bound or tied up.

Metallophobia- Fear of metal.

Metathesiophobia- Fear of changes.

Methyphobia- Fear of alcohol.

Microbiophobia- Fear of microbes. (Bacillophobia)

Microphobia- Fear of small things.

Misophobia or Mysophobia- Fear of being

contaminated with dirt or germs.

Mnemophobia- Fear of memories.

Molysmophobia or Molysomophobia- Fear of dirt or contamination.

Monophobia- Fear of solitude or being alone.

Monopathophobia- Fear of definite disease.

Motorphobia- Fear of automobiles.

Mottephobia- Fear of moths.

Musophobia or Muriphobia- Fear of mice.

Mycophobia- Fear or aversion to mushrooms.

Mycrophobia- Fear of small things.

Myctophobia- Fear of darkness.

Myrmecophobia- Fear of ants.

Mythophobia- Fear of myths or stories or false statements.

Myxophobia- Fear of slime. (Blennophobia)

Nebulaphobia- Fear of fog. (Homichlophobia)

Necrophobia- Fear of death or dead things.

Nelophobia- Fear of glass.

Neophobia- Fear of anything new.

Noctiphobia- Fear of the night.

Nomatophobia- Fear of names.

Nosocomephobia- Fear of hospitals.

Nosophobia or Nosemaphobia- Fear of becoming ill.

Nudophobia- Fear of nudity.

Numerophobia- Fear of numbers.

Nyctohylophobia- Fear of dark wooded areas or of forests at night

Nyctophobia- Fear of the dark or of night.

Obesophobia- Fear of gaining weight.

(Pocrescophobia)
Ochlophobia- Fear of crowds or mobs.
Ochophobia- Fear of vehicles.
Odontophobia- Fear of teeth or dental surgery.
Odynophobia or Odynephobia- Fear of pain.
(Algophobia)
Oikophobia- Fear of home surroundings,
house.(Domatophobia, Eicophobia)
Olfactophobia- Fear of smells.
Ombrophobia- Fear of rain or of being rained on.
Ommetaphobia or Ommatophobia- Fear of eyes.
Oneirophobia- Fear of dreams.
Oneirogmophobia- Fear of wet dreams.
Onomatophobia- Fear of hearing a certain word or of
names.
Ophidiophobia- Fear of snakes. (Snakephobia)
Ophthalmophobia- Fear of being stared at.
Opiophobia- Fear medical doctors experience of
prescribing needed pain medications for patients.
Optophobia- Fear of opening one's eyes.
Ornithophobia- Fear of birds.
Osmophobia or Osphresiophobia- Fear of smells or
odours.
Ostraconophobia- Fear of shellfish.
Ouranophobia or Uranophobia- Fear of heaven.

Pagophobia- Fear of ice or frost.
Panthophobia- Fear of suffering and disease.
Panophobia or Pantophobia- Fear of everything.
Papyrophobia- Fear of paper.
Paralipophobia- Fear of neglecting duty or

responsibility.

Parasitophobia- Fear of parasites.

Paraskavedekatriaphobia- Fear of Friday the 13th.

Parthenophobia- Fear of virgins or young girls.

Pathophobia- Fear of disease.

Parturiphobia- Fear of childbirth.

Peccatophobia- Fear of sinning or imaginary crimes.

Pediculophobia- Fear of lice.

Pediophobia- Fear of dolls.

Peniaphobia- Fear of poverty.

Phagophobia- Fear of swallowing or of eating or of being eaten.

Phallophobia- Fear of a penis, especially erect.

Pharmacophobia- Fear of taking medicine.

Phasmophobia- Fear of ghosts.

Phengophobia- Fear of daylight or sunshine.

Philemaphobia or Philematophobia- Fear of kissing.

Philophobia- Fear of falling in love or being in love.

Phobophobia- Fear of phobias.

Photoaugliaphobia- Fear of glaring lights.

Photophobia- Fear of light.

Phonophobia- Fear of noises or voices or one's own voice

Phthiriophobia- Fear of lice. (Pediculophobia)

Phthisiophobia- Fear of tuberculosis.

Plutophobia- Fear of wealth.

Pluviophobia- Fear of rain or of being rained on.

Pneumatiphobia- Fear of spirits.

Pnigophobia or Pnigerophobia- Fear of choking or being smothered.

Pocrescophobia- Fear of gaining weight.

(Obesophobia)

Polyphobia- Fear of many things.

Poinephobia- Fear of punishment.

Ponophobia- Fear of overworking or of pain.

Potamophobia- Fear of rivers or running water.

Potophobia- Fear of alcohol.

Pharmacophobia- Fear of drugs.

Proctophobia- Fear of rectums.

Prosophobia- Fear of progress.

Psellismophobia- Fear of stuttering.

Psychophobia- Fear of mind.

Psychrophobia- Fear of cold.

Pteromerhanophobia- Fear of flying.

Pupaphobia – Fear of puppets.

Pyrexiophobia- Fear of Fever.

Pyrophobia- Fear of fire.


Ranidaphobia- Fear of frogs.

Rhabdophobia- Fear of being severely punished or beaten by a rod, or of being severely criticised. Also fear of magic. (wand)

Rhypophobia- Fear of defecation.

Rhytiphobia- Fear of getting wrinkles.

Rupophobia- Fear of dirt.


Sarmassophobia- Fear of love play. (Malaxophobia)

Scabiophobia- Fear of scabies.

Scatophobia- Fear of faeces

Sciophobia & Sciaphobia- Fear of shadows.

Scoleciphobia- Fear of worms.

Scolionophobia- Fear of school.

Scopophobia or Scoptophobia- Fear of being seen or stared at.

Scotomaphobia- Fear of blindness in visual field.

Scotophobia- Fear of darkness. (Achluophobia)

Scriptophobia- Fear of writing in public.

Selachophobia- Fear of sharks.

Selaphobia- Fear of light flashes.

Selenophobia- Fear of the moon.

Seplophobia- Fear of decaying matter.

Sesquipedalophobia- Fear of long words.

Sexophobia- Fear of the opposite sex. (Heterophobia)

Siderodromophobia- Fear of trains, railroads or train travel.

Sinistrophobia- Fear of things to the left or left-handed.

Sinophobia- Fear of Chinese, Chinese culture.

Sitophobia or Sitiophobia- Fear of food or eating. (Cibophobia)

Snakephobia- Fear of snakes. (Ophidiophobia)

Social Phobia- Fear of being evaluated negatively in social situations.

Sociophobia- Fear of society or people in general.

Somniphobia- Fear of sleep.

Sophophobia- Fear of learning.

Soteriophobia – Fear of dependence on others.

Spacephobia- Fear of outer space.

Spectrophobia- Fear of spectres or ghosts.

Spermatophobia or Spermophobia- Fear of germs.

Spheksophobia- Fear of wasps.

Staurophobia- Fear of crosses or the crucifix.

Stenophobia- Fear of narrow things or places.

Stygiophobia or Stigiophobia- Fear of hell.

Suriphobia- Fear of mice.

Symbolophobia- Fear of symbolism.

Symmetrophobia- Fear of symmetry.

Syngenesophobia- Fear of relatives.

Syphilophobia- Fear of syphilis.

Tachophobia- Fear of speed.

Taeniophobia or Teniophobia- Fear of tapeworms.

Taphephobia Taphophobia- Fear of being buried alive or of cemeteries.

Tapinophobia- Fear of being contagious.

Taurophobia- Fear of bulls.

Technophobia- Fear of technology.

Teleophobia- 1) Fear of definite plans. 2) Religious ceremony.

Telephonophobia- Fear of telephones.

Testophobia- Fear of taking tests.

Tetanophobia- Fear of lockjaw, tetanus.

Textophobia- Fear of certain fabrics.

Thalassophobia- Fear of the sea.

Thanatophobia or Thantophobia- Fear of death or dying.

Theatrophobia- Fear of theatres.

Theologicophobia- Fear of theology.

Theophobia- Fear of gods or religion.

Thermophobia- Fear of heat.

Tocophobia- Fear of pregnancy or childbirth.

Tomophobia- Fear of surgical operations.

Tonitrophobia- Fear of thunder.

Topophobia- Fear of certain places or situations, such

as stage fright.

Toxiphobia or Toxophobia or Toxicophobia- Fear of poison or of being accidently poisoned.

Traumatophobia- Fear of injury.

Tremophobia- Fear of trembling.

Trichopathophobia or Trichophobia- Fear of hair. (Chaetophobia, Hypertrichophobia)

Triskaidekaphobia- Fear of the number 13.

Tropophobia- Fear of moving or making changes.

Trypanophobia- Fear of injections.

Uranophobia or Ouranophobia- Fear of heaven.

Urophobia- Fear of urine or urinating.

Venustraphobia- Fear of beautiful women.

Verbophobia- Fear of words.

Verminophobia- Fear of germs.

Vestiphobia- Fear of clothing.

Vitricophobia- Fear of step-father.

Wiccaphobia: Fear of witches and witchcraft.

Xanthophobia- Fear of the colour yellow or the word yellow.

Xenoglossophobia- Fear of foreign languages.

Xenophobia- Fear of strangers or foreigners.

Xerophobia- Fear of dryness.

Xylophobia- 1) Fear of wooden objects. 2) Forests.

Xyrophobia-Fear of razors.

Zelophobia- Fear of jealousy.

Zeusophobia- Fear of God or gods.

# APPENDIX

Zoophobia- Fear of animals.

# Bibliography

Successful Hypnotherapy by Neil French

Introductory Lectures on Psychoanalysis Lecture 24, The Common Neurotic State by Sigmund Freud

Introductory Lectures on Psychoanalysis by Sigmund Freud

The Toltec Path of Recapitulation by Victor Sanchez

Science of Being and Art of Living, Transcendental Meditation by Maharishi Mahesh Yogi

The Power of Intention by Dr Wayne Dyer

Oceans of Energy, The Patterns & Techniques of EmoTrance, Volume 1 by Dr Silvia Hartmann

Printed in Great Britain
by Amazon

54454853R00106